Court
on Trial

Celebrating 35 Years of
Penguin Random House India

Court on Trial

A Data-Driven
Account of the
Supreme
Court of
India

Aparna Chandra
Sital Kalantry
William H. J. Hubbard

PENGUIN
VIKING
An imprint of Penguin Random House

VIKING

USA | Canada | UK | Ireland | Australia
New Zealand | India | South Africa | China | Singapore

Viking is part of the Penguin Random House group of companies
whose addresses can be found at global.penguinrandomhouse.com

Published by Penguin Random House India Pvt. Ltd
4th Floor, Capital Tower 1, MG Road,
Gurugram 122 002, Haryana, India

Penguin
Random House
India

First published in Viking by Penguin Random House India 2023

The views and opinions expressed in this book are the authors' own and the
facts are as reported by them which have been verified to the extent possible,
and the publishers are not in any way liable for the same.

ISBN 9780670091584

Typeset in Adobe Garamond Pro by Manipal Technologies Limited, Manipal
Printed at Thomson Press India Ltd, New Delhi

www.penguin.co.in

*This book is dedicated to Professor Theodore Eisenberg (1947–2014),
a pioneer of empirical legal studies, whose work launched this project
and many other studies of courts around the world*

Contents

Introduction

It is often said of the Supreme Court of India that it is the most powerful court in the world.[1] Whether that statement is true or not, it is indeed the case that the Court exercises jurisdiction over a billion-plus people. It also has extensive powers—some explicitly mentioned in the Constitution, others acquired over time—which the Court wields frequently, if unevenly, in deciding cases, determining relief and monitoring implementation of its orders. It can invalidate acts of the executive, laws passed by the Parliament and even amendments to the Indian Constitution. The Court does not have to wait for a litigant to bring a case. In certain matters, it can take up a case *suo moto*—on its own. The Court can appoint *amicus curiae*—friends of the Court—to assist the Court in a case before it. It can set up its own fact-finding commissions or expert committees to help in decision-making. And through the use of extensive contempt powers, the Court can, if the judges so desire, force the State to comply with its orders.

Yet, despite its great authority and power, the Court is in crisis. In the seven decades since its creation, the Court has grown in size and power, but these changes have also spawned endemic problems and controversies. How should judges be appointed? What posts should they hold or not hold after retirement? What kinds of matters should the Court hear or prioritize? How should cases be allocated between different benches? Does the Court hear too few cases or too many? Should the Court have more judges? Should it have branches? Why do cases take so long and what can be done about it? Is the Court accessible to the common person and can it be more so? These are just some of the many questions about the Court and its working that have been debated recently.

Lawyers, judges, politicians and academics have proposed a range of policy proposals to address these problems—abolish two-judge benches,[2] set up special thematic benches,[3] establish regional benches,[4] bifurcate the Court's constitutional court function from its appellate court function,[5] change the system of appointment of judges,[6] require a 'cooling-off' period before judges can hold a political appointment post-retirement and curtail the Chief Justice's powers to allocate cases to benches, etc.[7] Underlying all of these discussions is a sense that something needs to change—'business as usual' is not enough. It is not surprising then that in recent times, every Chief Justice of India has started their tenure promising court reform—though their intentions have not always translated into actions.

What *is* surprising is that despite widespread agreement that the Court needs reform, there has been little effort to systematically plan this process. Many of the current reform proposals that are being debated within legal circles are based on impressionistic accounts and anecdotal evidence, rather than robust data-driven diagnoses or solutions. In fact, for an institution that wields so much power and impacts the lives, liberties and material circumstances of so many, there is very little quantitative research on the Court's structure, process and functions.[8]

This book responds to the need for hard data on the Court. We use empirical data to diagnose crises facing the Supreme Court and propose an ambitious but practical agenda for reform. In the chapters that follow, we identify six major areas of concern with the Court's functioning. And for each of those areas of concern, we ask questions, examine the data for answers and use these insights to offer suggestions for reform.

We will preview each of these areas of concern in more detail later in this Introduction, but for now, consider the following questions:

Does the Court make access for disadvantaged groups a priority, as it claims it does? In Chapter 1, we demonstrate that judges' well-intentioned efforts to provide wide access to the *Supreme Court* has perversely limited their ability to provide access to *justice*, especially for under-resourced groups.

How backlogged is the Court? How does delay factor into the incentives and disincentives of parties to litigate further? Chapter 2 describes the extent to which the Court's backlog gives life to the adage, 'justice delayed is justice denied'.

Do some lawyers have an advantage in getting their cases heard by the Court? Chapter 3 provides evidence that some lawyers are so influential that the Court gives them more hearings, even when they bring weaker cases.

Are cases randomly assigned to judges at the Supreme Court, or do Chief Justices strategically assign cases to influence how they are decided? Chapter 4 provides evidence that Chief Justices influence the outcomes of important cases by using their administrative powers of case assignment.

Have the judges of the Supreme Court used their power over the appointment of new judges to increase diversity in the Court? Chapter 5 demonstrates the subtle ways in which the judges of the Supreme Court have made the Court less—not more—diverse over time.

Does the early retirement age for judges—at sixty-five years of age—impact their work? Chapter 6 demonstrates that short tenures at the Court and early retirement produce institutional instability as well as perverse incentives for judges to 'pander' to the government of the day.

These questions matter in understanding the functioning of the Supreme Court, deciding whether it needs reform and determining the trajectories of such reform. More importantly, every one of these questions depend on empirical data about cases, judges and lawyers, which this book provides.

Our Approach

This book brings together insights from five new, unique datasets based on records from over one million Supreme Court cases, the text of thousands of Supreme Court judgments, biographical information on hundreds of Supreme Court justices and high court judges, and data on senior advocates at the Supreme Court. It also incorporates innovative work by many other exceptional empirical scholars. It supplements the empirical data with insights gained from our own extensive interviews with Supreme Court justices, lawyers and academics. (At the end of this introductory chapter, we provide details on our process of creating the datasets used in this book.)

Nonetheless, our methods cannot address every question about the Court. There are many crises facing the Indian judiciary—this book focuses on crises that can be examined through empirical data that currently exists and our suggestions for reform are limited to these areas. We do not claim to address every possibility for reform, or every current crisis in the Court. Ultimately, the test of a well-functioning judicial system is whether it consistently delivers just outcomes. No one book or research methodology can fully answer this question. We bring one lens to this inquiry—do the institutional and administrative structures and processes of the Court aid or impede its ability to deliver just outcomes?

We also would like to emphasize that although the Supreme Court of India sits on a *global* stage and its actions have ramifications around the world, it is an *Indian* institution. It is a central pillar of India's polity and should be accountable to the people of India. Though two of the three authors of this book are not citizens or residents of India, we have all devoted years to researching the Indian Supreme Court; we have each walked the corridors of the Court, interviewed its justices and other staff and crunched the numbers in our data on the Court's cases. We believe that as the trustee of such extensive public powers, the Supreme Court of India requires continuous public scrutiny of its functioning. A range of perspectives and voices are essential to a fully informed and democratic debate about the future of the Court. We hope to add to this debate by providing a data-driven assessment of the Court's functioning.

In the remainder of this chapter, we provide an introductory overview of the history, structure and processes of the Indian Supreme

Court. We also highlight areas of concern in the Court's functioning and explain the structure of the book. At the end, we describe our data sources and the creation of the five new datasets that inform our analysis in the chapters that follow.

Overview: A Court in Crisis

Soul of the Constitution?

The Supreme Court sits atop a broadly three-tiered judicial system, comprising the district-level civil and criminal courts, high courts and the Supreme Court. Various specialized tribunals also feed cases into the judicial system, often directly into the Supreme Court.[9] The Indian judicial system is unitary, that is, all courts can decide cases pertaining to state as well as central laws. Decisions of the Supreme Court are binding on all courts within the territory of India.[10]

The Supreme Court performs a dual function—first, it can be approached directly to decide a range of constitutional disputes such as those relating to the violation of fundamental rights, disputes between the Centre and states or between states, disputes relating to the election of high functionaries, etc.[11] In these matters, the Court exercises original jurisdiction, that is, a petitioner can approach the Supreme Court directly to seek remedy for such constitutional violations. The most frequently invoked part of the Court's original jurisdiction is the power under Article 32 of the Constitution, which guarantees the right to move the Court, by way of a writ petition, to enforce fundamental rights. The Chairperson of the Drafting Committee of the Indian Constitution, B. R. Ambedkar, described Article 32 as the most important provision of the Constitution and called it the 'very soul of the Constitution and the very heart of it', without which the Constitution would be a 'nullity',[12] implying that protecting fundamental rights is the most important function of the Supreme Court. However, by 2011 writ petitions were only 8 per cent of the Court's admitted and disposed cases.[13] The vast majority of the Court's workload is devoted to cases that do not involve fundamental rights.

Perhaps the most high-profile component of the Court's docket is Public Interest Litigation (PIL). Since the late 1970s, the Supreme Court has allowed any public spirited person to approach the Court on behalf of any person whose fundamental rights have been violated but who cannot, 'by reason of poverty, helplessness or disability or socially or economically disadvantaged position', come before the Court for relief themselves.[14] Today, PILs are filed on a range of governance-related issues and are so often reported in the press that from a perusal of the news and social media, one may come away with the impression that PILs form a significant part of the Court's docket. It may be surprising to learn, that only about 3 per cent of the reported judgments of the Court deal with PIL matters.[15]

The Supreme Court also sits as an appellate court. It is the final court of appeal for orders passed by any court or tribunal in the country on any type of matter—civil or criminal. It can entertain appeals in three ways. First, high courts may certify a case for appeal to the Supreme Court.[16] Second, statutes may provide for direct appeals to the Supreme Court from orders or judgments delivered by other courts or by tribunals.[17] And finally, under Article 136 of the Constitution, the Court has a very broad discretionary power to grant 'special leave to appeal from any judgment, decree, determination, sentence or order in any cause or matter passed or made by any court or tribunal in the territory of India'.[18] This broad discretionary appellate power was initially conceived as a residuary exceptional power to be exercised sparingly and with caution.[19] However, today, the 'special leave petition' or SLP route is the most preferred means to appeal to the Supreme Court, aided by an expansive interpretation of this jurisdiction by the Supreme Court itself.[20] Appeals, the bulk of them SLPs, currently comprise approximately 92.4 per cent of the Court's entire docket,[21] and about 88 per cent of its docket of admitted and disposed matters.[22] Less than 4 per cent of the appellate docket (of admitted cases) relates to constitutional matters.[23]

Overall, the Court's constitutional jurisdiction, especially its power to remedy violations of fundamental rights—described by the framers as the most important provision of the entire Constitution—forms a small and shrinking part of the Court's workload. PILs, though very high-profile, are a tiny share of the docket. The bulk of the Court's docket comprises civil and criminal, but not constitutional, appeals under the SLP jurisdiction. This has led to an 'identity crisis' in the Supreme Court—is it primarily a constitutional court or a court of appeals?[24]

The Supreme Courts of India

The Supreme Court of today is very different from what it was at the founding of the Republic, both in its structure and in its powers. When the first judges of the Supreme Court were sworn in on 28 January 1950, two days after India became a constitutional republic, the Court had eight seats, six of which were filled. The very first case on the interpretation of the Constitution that the judges heard was *A. K. Gopalan v. The State of Madras*.[25] The State had detained Gopalan, a prominent Communist leader, under the Preventive Detention Act, 1950. Gopalan challenged the constitutionality of this law before the Supreme Court. All six judges sat together to hear the case. Though the entire Court rarely sat together, i.e., sat *en banc*, this practice of sitting in large benches that comprised nearly all members of the Court would remain common in the initial years, as the number of cases on the Court's docket was low.[26] In 1950, the six (later seven) judges of the Supreme Court considered whether or not to admit 1037 cases[27] and issued forty-three judgments.[28] Since then, the workload of the Court has been increasing exponentially. At present, the Court has thirty-four seats,[29] entertains over 60,000 appeals and petitions,[30] and issues approximately 1000 judgments per year.[31]

To keep up with its expanding docket, the Court sits in much smaller benches—most frequently in benches of two judges, sometimes three and rarely five or more judges. In fact, though the Constitution requires the Court to sit in Constitution Benches (i.e., benches of five or more judges) to decide 'substantial questions of law as to the interpretation of the Constitution',[32] the Court frequently sits in smaller benches, even for significant constitutional matters. This was the case with *Suresh Kumar Koushal*,[33] the infamous 2013 decision, where a two-judge bench of the Supreme Court reversed the Delhi High Court and upheld the constitutionality of Section 377 Indian Penal Code (IPC), which criminalized sodomy. If ever there was a matter that required the Supreme Court to decide upon the interpretation of the Constitution, it was this matter, pertaining to the rights and protections guaranteed by the Constitution to a range of sexual minorities. Similarly, in *Subramanian Swamy v. Union of India*,[34] a two-judge bench decided and dismissed a challenge to the constitutionality of criminal defamation, while acknowledging that the case raised significant concerns regarding the freedom of speech and expression guaranteed by the Constitution. This practice of deciding matters of significant constitutional import by benches of two or three judges is a common occurrence. Constitution Benches have declined in frequency from an average of seventy-one per year in the first twenty-five years of the Constitution, to only eleven per year in the next twenty-five.[35] In the period between 2010 and 2015, 78 per cent of the constitutional challenges before the Court were decided by two-judge benches.[36]

Working in smaller benches might be efficient to deal with the large number of incoming cases, but this has a negative impact on some of the core characteristics of the Indian legal system. After Independence, India continued with the 'common law' legal system. Under the common law system, a court lower in hierarchy from the Supreme Court is bound by the judgments of the Supreme Court.[37] The Supreme Court itself is bound by its previous decisions—its precedents—except in rare cases when previously settled questions of law can be reopened. The common law system assumes that the legal universe is made up of consistent rules that can be applied uniformly to cases which present similar or analogous facts as the precedent where the rule was settled.

However, a result of having multiple benches of the Supreme Court dealing with similar issues and laying down rules is that each bench of the Court speaks for the entire court, but all the benches do not necessarily speak with one voice. This can result in conflicting precedents coming from the Supreme Court, which then lead not only to confusion for future courts and courts lower down the hierarchy, but also end up generating avoidable litigation since applicable rules are not clear to anyone. The Court has created rules to minimize such conflicts and secure uniformity in decisions rendered by different benches. For example, a bench of the Supreme Court is generally bound by the decision of a previous bench of the same or larger size. If it doubts the validity of such a prior decision, it has to refer the matter to the Chief Justice of India, who will constitute a larger bench to examine the issue.[38] Despite such rules, conflicting precedents from different benches of the Supreme Court are a frequent occurrence.

The litigation around the interpretation of Section 24 of the Right to Fair Compensation and Transparency in Land Acquisition, Rehabilitation and Resettlement Act, 2013 (LARR Act) exemplifies these concerns. The LARR Act was a successor to the colonial and much criticized Land Acquisition Act of 1894. Section 24 deals with legacy issues arising from pending proceedings under the old Act and lists the instances where landowners in such pending proceedings would be entitled to the (much higher) rates of compensation under the 2013 Act.

In 2014, when the new law came into force, the State sought a restricted interpretation of this provision so that they would not have to provide such enhanced compensation. In January 2014, in the case of *Pune Municipal Corporation v. Harakchand Misirimal Solanki,*[39] a three-judge bench of the Supreme Court disagreed with the State. Various benches of the Supreme Court and high courts across the country applied this decision to subsequent litigation. In 2016, a two-judge bench of the Supreme Court even recognized *Pune Municipal Corporation* to be the ruling precedent on this point.[40] However, in December 2017, another two-judge bench doubted the correctness of *Pune Municipal Corporation.*[41] Since a smaller bench could not overrule the decision of a larger bench, it asked the Chief Justice to constitute a larger bench to consider whether *Pune Municipal Corporation* required a relook. The Chief Justice constituted a three-judge bench to decide the matter—the same bench size as in *Pune Municipal Corporation.* In February 2018, in *Indore Development Authority v. Shailendra,*[42] this new bench held that *Pune Municipal Corporation* was wrongly decided. As stated earlier, a three-judge bench cannot overrule the decision of another three-judge bench. *Indore Development Authority* got around this problem by declaring the decision in *Pune Municipal Corporation* to be *per incuriam*—so bad in law, that it had no legal effect at all. In other words, *Pune Municipal Corporation* was not a valid precedent and it did not bind the Court in *Indore Development Authority*. This new bench held in favour of the interpretation advanced by the state. Two questions arose immediately—(1) in the context of the dispute at hand, which interpretation of Section 24—the one accepted in *Pune Municipal Corporation* or the one in *Indore Development Authority*—was to be followed? and (2) as a larger issue, could a later bench declare the decision of a previous bench of the same size to be *per incuriam*? What impact would this have on the system of precedents upon which the edifice of the Indian judicial system is (at least purportedly) built? Different benches referred both questions to the Chief Justice and asked him to constitute an even larger bench—this time of five judges. In March 2020, this five-judge bench upheld the *Indore Development Authority* interpretation of Section 24.[43]

While the entire saga of the litigation around Section 24, LARR Act, might appear to be an egregious example of the manner in which the Court can speak in multiple voices within a short span of time, this instance is not a complete outlier. A more routine example comes from the Court's death penalty jurisprudence where different contemporaneous benches have applied very different standards for determining when death penalty should be imposed.[44] Cases such as these capture the multiple voices in which the Supreme Court may speak at the same time, putting paid to the notion that the Court is a singular institution bound by the dictates of precedents. This 'poly-vocality'[45] of the Supreme Court leaves lower courts and the general public uncertain about the applicable rules, impacting the certainty and predictability of the law, and in the case of the death penalty, leaving judges unguided in deciding questions of life and death.

In Chapter 1, we examine the workload of the Supreme Court and argue that the Court's impulse to provide increased access to the

Supreme Court, while well-intentioned, counter-intuitively limits access to justice across the board. For most Indians, access to justice means access to trial courts, tribunals and maybe the high courts. It does not mean access to the Supreme Court. Improving access to justice requires making it easier for the impoverished and disadvantaged to get a hearing and just outcomes, in one of the thousands of lower courts and tribunals. The Court can aid such access by focusing its resources on announcing clear legal rules and promptly adjudicating important or difficult questions of law. By answering these questions, the Court could give clear guidance to the lower courts on how they should decide the millions of cases on their docket, hold the state accountable for its transgressions and thus improve the quality of outcomes across the judicial system.

Tareekh pe Tareekh[46]

Access to justice through courts for the common person is impacted by the amount of time courts take to decide cases. Delay in decision-making is endemic in the Indian judiciary. In the trial courts of India, roughly one in eleven cases have been pending for more than ten years.[47]

Extensive delays in deciding disputes often crowd out people who cannot afford to spend years in court. This is why, perhaps, lawyers on the ground sometimes suggest that 'if you have a strong case, settle; if you have a weak case, go to court'. Going to court and delaying the settlement of a dispute aids the party with the weaker case to postpone legal liability. It may push parties with fewer resources but stronger cases to settle for less or to give up their claim entirely. Delay then favours the well-resourced but legally weaker party.

There are many reasons for delays in the Indian judicial system. Too many cases and too few judges are one part of the problem. In addition, the institutional and working culture of courts—where dilatory tactics are not only an accepted part of court craft, but find willing acceptance from judges—plays a significant role in keeping the judicial system backlogged. It is not surprising then, that of the reasons recorded for delays in trial courts on the Supreme Court's National

Judicial Data Grid, seeking intervention and stay by higher courts, non-availability of counsel, important witnesses not turning up, and blocking proceedings by filing repeated applications, are some of the most common.[48]

In India, delay has often been seen as a lower court problem.[49] If anything, the problem is worse at the high court level. Approximately one in five cases at the high-court level has been pending for more than ten years. Nearly 15 per cent of the writ petitions for the enforcement of fundamental rights, or for the performance of public functions or statutory or public duties,[50] have been pending at the high courts for more than ten years.[51]

The Supreme Court does not even provide the age-wise breakup of its own cases on the National Judicial Data Grid, which has been put in place by the Supreme Court itself. Our data suggests that as of March 2018, one in nearly thirteen cases on the Supreme Court's docket had been pending for over ten years, and additionally more than one in three cases on the docket had been pending for over five years.[52] Of the disposed cases,[53] the median case (that is, half the cases) are disposed of in approximately one and a half years from filing. However, the average time that the Court takes for disposal is approximately two and a half years. By itself, this might not sound like a long time. But if half the cases are taking less than a year and a half, and the average case is taking two and a half years, this implies that at the top end, the delay is so high that the average is being pulled up. This can be seen from the fact that the fastest one-fifth (20th percentile) of the cases took only eighty-nine days (or around three months) from filing to disposal after admission whereas the slowest one-fifths (the 80th percentile) took about four years and four months from filing to disposal. The slowest of cases, at the 95th percentile, took about eight years and three months to disposal. Overall, the Supreme Court appears to provide a two-track justice—super fast disposals to some cases and long gestation for others.

The Supreme Court then does not fare much better than lower courts on the metric of delay. On average, a case takes thirteen years and six months from filing in the Court of first instance to a decision on merits by the Supreme Court.[54] The Court itself accounts for about one-third of this total, approximately on a par with the average amount of time taken at each tier of the judiciary.[55] The extent of delay in the Indian judicial system, particularly at the Supreme Court, and its causes, consequences and possible solutions, are discussed in Chapter 2.

From the Chamber of Princes to the Peoples' Court—And Back Again?

With over 60,000 petitions filed in the Supreme Court annually, a large part of the Court's time goes into deciding which of these cases should be admitted. Admission of cases tends to take place over two rounds. One, on first being listed before the Court, the bulk of cases are dismissed outright—or in legal parlance, dismissed *in limine*. For those that remain, the Court very rarely admits the matter without giving the other side an opportunity to be heard. Generally, most cases move to round two where the Court issues notice to the other side and may stay the operation of the action against which the case has been filed. On receipt of notice, the other side appears and may argue why the case should not be admitted by the Court. After hearing the other side, the Court generally does one of three things: it may dismiss the matter after listening to both parties; it may admit the matter and decide it based on the brief hearing during the admissions process; or it may list the matter for a regular, more detailed hearing on merits. A litigant can also pre-emptively file a 'caveat' before the Court, requesting that no petition be admitted in a given matter without first hearing that litigant. Where a caveat has been filed, the matter is listed for admission only after notice is served to such party. In the period between 2015 and 2019 (both inclusive), the Court admitted 12.8 per cent, or roughly one in every eight cases in which it decided on the admission application.[56]

Every Monday and Friday, judges sitting in benches of two, hear up to sixty fresh admission cases and 'after notice' matters. Tuesdays, Wednesdays and Thursdays are generally reserved for regular hearings. However, since the burden of admission matters is so large, in recent times, the Court has been listing 'after notice' matters, especially those

at the stage of final disposal, on the regular hearing days as well.[57] To
go through so many fresh admission matters, judges have very few
minutes to spare on each case: on average ninety-three seconds.[58] In
such a case, the 'face value' of the lawyer appearing for the parties
assumes great importance in persuading the judge to admit the matter.
The impact of the *uber*-expensive elite bar, especially those designated
senior advocates, on the admissions process, is discussed in Chapter 3.
Suffice to say, if access to the portals of the Supreme Court is mediated
by access to an expensive lawyer, then the Court is not really accessible
to the bulk of the population.

   This issue of access—or rather lack thereof—to the Court has been
a constant concern throughout the Court's history. For the first eight
years of its existence, the Supreme Court sat in the Chamber of Princes
in the Parliament building. This Chamber was originally constructed
in colonial times to serve as a forum to convene and voice the interest of
princes who were under the suzerainty of the British Raj. The Chamber
of Princes—and what it represented—serves as a metaphor for abiding
concerns with the Supreme Court's priorities. Through the first three
decades of its existence, the Court faced repeated criticisms that it was
a forum for 'legal quibbling of men with long purses'.[59] To change this
perception, starting the late 1970s, judges of the Court engaged in a
deliberate exercise to make it a People's Court, in terms of easy access,
priorities in the kinds of matters it dealt with, and its jurisprudence.
After liberalization at the start of the 1990s, the Court has again
come in for criticism that, much like the World-Bank-led structural
adjustment of the Indian economy, the Supreme Court engaged in a
'structural adjustment of judicial review', and has aligned its priorities
in ways that disempower the most marginalized.[60] What does data have
to say about the Court's self-understanding as a People's Court? We
discuss this in Chapter 1.

The Master's Roster

As discussed above, the Supreme Court today sees more cases coming
before it being decided by judges sitting in smaller benches. Who gets

to decide which judge hears what case? This is a role for the Chief Justice of India. The Chief Justice is the Master of the Roster, which means that the Chief Justice, and the Chief Justice alone, determines who will hear what case. Most cases are assigned in a routine fashion, based on a now formal roster of subject-wise allocation of cases to judges. However, at times, the Chief Justice has to assign a specific case to a specific set of judges. This typically happens in the most salient cases where the Chief Justice has to set up larger benches to hear specific matters for reasons such as resolving conflicting or doubtful precedent—like in *Indore Development Authority* above,[61] or setting up Constitution Benches to decide substantial questions as to the interpretation of the Constitution.[62] The exercise of this Master of the Roster power has become extremely contentious in recent years, even leading up to an impeachment motion in 2018 against a Chief Justice of India—Justice Dipak Misra.[63] The Section 24, LARR Act controversy discussed above, itself exemplifies concerns with the application of this power. The two-judge bench that doubted the interpretation in *Pune Municipal Corporation* was headed by Justice Arun Mishra. When he referred the matter to the Chief Justice to constitute a larger bench, the Chief Justice assigned Justice Mishra to head the three-judge bench that went on to hold that *Pune Municipal Corporation* was *per incuriam.* When the Chief Justice had to constitute a five-judge bench to consider whether *Indore Development Authority* was right in its interpretation of Section 24, and whether it was right in declaring the decision of a coordinate bench to be *per incuriam,* the Chief Justice *again* assigned Justice Mishra to head this bench. The Chief Justice's role in bench formation in these cases was the latest in a long and growing list of concerns around the scope and application of the Master of the Roster power. We discuss this issue in detail in Chapter 4.

Consultation, Concurrence, Collegium, Commission

Underlying the Master of the Roster controversy is the understanding that who the judge is plays an important role in how the case is decided. If all that judges did was apply objectively ascertainable facts to objectively determinable laws, then who the judge is would not matter very much. This understanding of the judicial role is no longer prevalent. Judges retain extensive discretion in deciding what are relevant facts, which of such facts have been proven, what inferences can be drawn from such facts, what are the applicable laws relevant to a case, what is the meaning of those laws, how those laws as interpreted apply to the facts as determined by the judge, what relief to provide to parties, etc. How judges exercise this discretion depends to a large extent on the judge's personal ideology, social location, life history, experiences and training.[64] This is why judges can, and do, disagree with each other on how a case should be decided.

If who is the judge is important, then the process of appointing judges to the Supreme Court assumes significance. The Constitution provides that judges of the Supreme Court will be appointed by the President of India in consultation with the Chief Justice of India and such other judges as the President may deem necessary.[65] Concerns were raised from the very beginning that the executive was trying to 'pack the Court' with its own appointees, thus harming the independence of the judiciary.[66] Though the Court was initially hesitant to interfere with the allocation of the appointment powers in the Constitution, in 1993 it determined that the requirement to 'consult' the Chief Justice meant that the President had to not only consult but seek the 'concurrence' of the Chief Justice. To ensure that the Chief Justice acts in an institutional capacity and not on personal whim, the Court established the 'collegium' system of appointments. In this system, a collegium consisting of the Chief Justice of India and the four senior-most judges of the Supreme Court initiates appointments to the Supreme Court. This recommendation is sent to the President, who, acting on the aid and advice of the Council of Ministers, can either accept the recommendation, or seek a reconsideration from the collegium. If the collegium reconsiders the recommendation and unanimously affirms the recommendation again, the President is bound to make the appointment. In 2015, the Supreme Court struck down a Constitutional Amendment that sought to transfer the appointment powers from the collegium to a National Judicial Appointments Commission.[67]

If a judge's social location and background influence judicial outcomes, then one would expect a robust appointments process to factor in social diversity as a relevant consideration in making appointments. On this parameter, the Supreme Court has failed significantly. To date, only eleven of the 266 judges who have served (or are currently serving) on the Supreme Court have been women. Only five appointees have belonged to the Scheduled Castes and only one person belonging to the Scheduled Tribes has ever been appointed to the Court. We discuss the appointments process and diversity on the bench in Chapter 5.

Pandering to the Political Branches?—Early Retirement and the Challenges of Judicial Independence

In 2020, four months after retiring as the Chief Justice of India, Justice Ranjan Gogoi sparked a furore when he accepted a nomination to the Rajya Sabha from the Government of India. Concerns about *quid pro quo* dodged this nomination and called into question his judgments, especially those delivered towards the end of his tenure.[68] It also highlighted concerns that an early retirement age for Supreme Court judges undermines judicial independence.

Judges of the Supreme Court retire at sixty-five years of age. However, as life expectancy has increased, judges are more likely to need post-retirement employment when they leave the Court, given that their pensions do not match their pre-retirement salaries and perks. This creates incentives to pander to those most likely to give them post-retirement jobs—government actors. Empirical evidence suggests that many Supreme Court judges do pander to the government as they get closer to retirement.[69] Not only does this call into question judicial independence, but it also harms the public perception of judicial impartiality. Further, the age at which judges are appointed to the Court and the age at which a judge becomes Chief Justice, has gone up over time. Since the retirement age has not changed, this means that the Chief Justices and judges themselves have shorter tenures than they did in the past. This creates institutional instability in terms of the management of the Court and maintenance of precedent. We discuss the issues raised by an early retirement age and propose reforms in Chapter 6.

An Agenda for Reform

Overall, the Supreme Court's institutional structures and processes are working at cross purposes with the Court's own aims and claims. While the Court seeks to be a 'people's court' that provides access to disadvantaged groups, its policies on admitting cases limits access to justice for the same groups. While the Court has a critical role in enforcing the state's constitutional accountability, its caseload of constitutional matters has been crowded out by routine appeals. While it seeks to provide timely justice, the backlog at the Supreme Court is as high as that in lower courts. While the Court claims to decide cases on the basis of the merits of the case, its decisions are impacted by extraneous consideration such as the stature of the lawyer, the allocation of cases by the Chief Justice, and judges' interest in seeking post-retirement sinecures for themselves. While in theory all judges wield equal power on the judicial side, the Chief Justice's administrative powers as Master of the Roster impacts outcomes of cases, and thus gives the Chief Justice primacy in judicial decision-making. And while the judiciary claims to work in the 'public interest', the lack of diversity on the bench limits its ability to take into account the interests of excluded groups.

On the basis of our research, we propose concrete changes to the structure and functioning of the Supreme Court to bring its working in alignment with its role and ambitions. The conclusion summarizes our reform proposals. We recognize that reforming a complex institution like the Supreme Court is no easy task. Suggestions for reform are easy to propose, but harder to execute. Some measures require the Parliament to act and others must come internally from the Court itself. Reform also threatens entrenched interests, including those of the bar. Reforming institutions requires leadership, vision and a willingness by the powerful to give up some of that power. Above all, it requires information and the will to change. We hope, that by shedding light on the working of the Court, this book will aid in the much-needed movement towards change.

Description of Methods and Data

Our data and methods in this book expand upon articles we have published in peer-reviewed academic journals around the world.[70] We also draw upon the important work of other researchers. We cite their work throughout this book, but we note here that key findings upon which we rely were made by scholars and research institutions, including George H. Garbois, Jr; Nick Robinson; Andrew Green and Albert Yoon; Rahul Hemrajani and Himanshu Agarwal; Madhav Aney, Shubhankar Dam and Giovanni Ko; the Bingham Centre for the Rule of Law and the Vidhi Centre for Legal Policy.

To their work, we add our own unique contributions, which take the form of five new and distinct databases, bringing together an unprecedented amount of information on the cases and judgments of the Supreme Court, and the judges and lawyers who heard and argued them. Below, we summarize each of the databases and our methods for collecting the data.

Supreme Court Opinions Dataset

This dataset is based on a comprehensive collection of all opinions of the Court from 2010 to 2015, as published in the case reporter Supreme Court Cases (SCC). The dataset contains 5699 judgments from 2010 to 2015 (dealing with 6857 cases). Our methodology for creating this dataset involved five roughly sequential elements: (1) selection of source material for Court opinions; (2) initial development of a template for hand coding and pilot testing, review and revision of the template; (3) comprehensive hand coding of all cases within the sample frame; (4) processing and quality control and (5) creation of the final database for analysis.

First, we selected SCC as the source material for our dataset because it is the most cited reporter by and before the Supreme Court. Since

SCC is a private reporter, it is under no obligation to publish every decision given by the Supreme Court. However, it is easily accessible, has extensive headnotes, and unlike other reporters, records many details, including the names and designations of lawyers involved.

Second, we developed an initial template identifying variables of interest that our research team could extract from written opinions of the Court. At this stage, students at Cornell Law School in the United States coded cases based on an initial template. After review of the pilot effort, the template was overhauled. To ensure internal consistency within the final dataset, we discarded the results of the pilot coding phase.

Third, we assembled a team of nearly two-dozen students from National Law University (NLU), Delhi, who then took up the task of coding cases. The team read judicial opinions from the SCC Reporter and completed Excel templates. The NLU Delhi team hand-coded all cases reported in SCC in its volumes for the years 2010 to 2015. Cases reported in these volumes that were decided prior to 2010 were excluded from consideration. Each case was coded for sixty-six variables.

Fourth, the team of coders at NLU Delhi then worked with a team of researchers at the University of Chicago Coase-Sandor Institute for Law and Economics to identify coding errors and variables that required recoding. This iterative process involved statistical analysis of the coded data to identify inconsistencies in coding patterns across variables. This primarily consisted of items being entered inconsistently by coders, due to spelling errors or the use of abbreviations by some coders but not others. These inconsistencies were documented by the research team and corrected through an automated recoding process to make codes consistent across cases.

We used the Stata software for statistical analysis. We thereafter converted the cleaned and processed data into Stata database format for statistical analysis. The dataset includes all Court judgments from 2010 through 2015 that have been published in the SCC, with the exception of orders from one-judge benches.

We used the Supreme Court Opinions Dataset to generate our results reported in Chapter 1, on how the Supreme Court is and is not a 'people's court'. We also used the Supreme Court Opinions Dataset (along with the Senior Advocates Dataset and Supreme Court Cases Dataset) to generate our results reported in Chapter 3, on the power and influence of senior advocates.[71] This dataset, along with the Supreme Court Justices dataset, also helped us analyse how Chief Justices use their Master of the Roster powers, which we discuss in Chapter 4.

Supreme Court Cases Dataset

This dataset is composed of information scraped from the Supreme Court of India website in November 2018. The data covered the years 2000 to 2018 and included more than one million pending and decided cases for which information is available on the Supreme Court website. The 'scraping' process involved going to the webpage http://supremecourtofindia.nic.in/case-status and then downloading all case information for each 'Court', 'State' and 'Year' tab on the website at the time (the website has since been redesigned). The downloaded information was saved in CSV (comma-separated values) files, which were then merged. For each case, these files provided information such as the Court from which the case originated, its state of origin, year of filing, diary number, case number and judgment date.

This data in turn allowed the downloading of additional case information based on diary number (a number assigned to cases by the Supreme Court for administrative purposes). This additional case information included information on the identities of the petitioner, respondent, their attorneys and information on the dates and outcomes of hearings.

We used the Supreme Court Cases Dataset to generate our results reported in Chapter 2, on the burden of backlogs in the Supreme Court.

Senior Advocates Dataset

This is a dataset of 466 civil cases filed in the Supreme Court in 2010. Each of these cases began as a special leave petition that was labelled in the Court's records as an 'ordinary civil matter' being appealed from the Delhi High Court. We followed the cases from admissions stage through to completion, with hand coding of advocate status. We chose this specific set of cases to ensure a sample of cases that were similar in terms of case type, origin and year, but which varied in terms of representation by advocates and senior advocates.

Information about the case history, case type, attorney names, hearing dates and hearing outcomes was drawn from the Supreme Court Cases Dataset. Each of these cases was then hand-coded to identify the status of the attorneys in the case (advocates or senior advocates) by our researcher Malavika Parthasarathy in early 2019.

We used the Senior Advocates Dataset (along with the Supreme Court Opinions Dataset and the Supreme Court Cases Dataset) to generate our results reported in Chapter 3, on the power and influence of senior advocates.

Supreme Court Justices Dataset

This dataset includes biographical information on all the judges appointed to the Supreme Court of India (SCI) from its founding to March 2018. With this dataset, we can compare the diversity of judges appointed during the pre-collegium period to the diversity of judges appointed since the onset of the collegium system in October 1993.

This dataset was created by student researchers based out of Cornell Law School and NLU Delhi using a template created by the authors to enter biographical information gleaned from the website of the SCI into an Excel spreadsheet. The authors then converted the data to Stata format for statistical analysis, conducted checks for coding errors and corrected ambiguities or errors in the coded data.

We used the Supreme Court Justices Dataset (along with the High Court chief justices Dataset) to generate our results reported in Chapter 5, on the diversity (or lack thereof) in judicial appointments.[72]

High Court Chief Justices Dataset

This dataset includes biographical information on all the chief justices of the high courts since 1993. As we show in Chapter 5, nearly all judges appointed to the SCI under the collegium were chief justices of their high courts. By studying the chief justices of the high courts, therefore, we are able to examine the characteristics of the single group of individuals most likely to be selected by the collegium for appointment to the SCI.

This dataset was created by a team of coders, research assistants of two of the authors, who were students at Cornell Law School and NLU Delhi. Each coder used a template created by the authors to enter biographical information gleaned from the websites of the high courts into an Excel spreadsheet. The coding teams at Cornell Law School and NLU Delhi worked independently to compile a comprehensive list of high court chief justices and enter their biographical attributes. One of the authors then compiled the spreadsheets, converted them to Stata format for statistical analysis and conducted checks for coding errors and inter-coder consistency. When necessary, the coders or the authors themselves identified and corrected ambiguities or errors in the coded data.

We used the High Court Chief Justices Dataset (along with the Supreme Court Justices Dataset) to generate our results reported in Chapter 5, on the diversity (or lack thereof) in judicial appointments.[73]

* * *

The data analysis for this book was completed in June 2020 and the information presented here is current to that date. While the pandemic did bring about changes in the working of the Courts—most notably the introduction of online hearings and live-streaming of court proceedings—the crises that we discuss in this book remain or have only worsened. Thus, the data and analysis in this book continue to be applicable to describe the Court today and speak to the ongoing conversation around court reform.

1

A 'People's Court'?

[T]his Court has always regarded the poor and the disadvantaged as entitled to preferential consideration than the rich and the affluent, the businessmen and the industrialists.[1]

The Supreme Court of India has long been thought of as a court for the common person. This perception is rooted in the Indian Constitution, which grants the Supreme Court original jurisdiction to hear cases alleging violations of fundamental rights.[2]

The Court itself has embraced this vision of its role. The words above come from a Supreme Court opinion in a case called *Bihar Legal Support Society v. Chief Justice of India* and the sentiments expressed have long permeated the rhetoric of the Supreme Court. It conceives of itself as an institution of 'last resort for the oppressed and bewildered'.[3] The Court's self-conscious pro-poor orientation is most evident in its public interest jurisprudence—the Court created a public interest litigation jurisdiction or PIL, through which it removed many procedural barriers to accessing the Court. Through PILs, activists can bring fundamental rights claims directly to the Court on behalf of individuals who do not have the resources to bring such claims on their own. Over the past several decades, the Court has exercised a wide-ranging authority to order remedies for a range of socio-economic injustices within its PIL jurisdiction.

But critics of the Court have claimed that at least since the 1990s, the Court has turned away from its commitment to protect the interests of marginalized groups.[4] Instead, some lawyers and legal scholars see the Court as supporting the interests of big businesses, at the expense of giving special attention to marginalized groups. As scholar and activist Usha Ramanathan argues, the poor and powerless no longer 'have the Court on their side'.[5]

What is the evidence for the view that the Court has lost interest in protecting the interests of the common person? Critics have pointed to the success rates of different types of parties in litigation in the Supreme Court—in other words, who wins more often when the Court decides a case. Critics note that over the past decade, if one looks at cases involving fundamental rights, the win rates for parties seeking to vindicate those rights in the Supreme Court have fallen over time.[6]

It is natural to interpret falling win rates for petitioners bringing certain rights-based claims as a sign that the Court is less of a 'people's court'. This may be true in some contexts, such as in the studies above which look at cases like PILs filed in the Supreme Court itself. But, as we will show in this chapter, data on another type of case—special leave petitions or SLPs, which make up the vast majority of the Court's caseload—may tell a different story about the Supreme Court.

Our research indicates that the Supreme Court is still a 'people's court', at least in one sense of the term. Our analysis of the data on Supreme Court cases provides evidence that the Court does give preferential treatment to the less powerful parties in litigation—individuals rather than corporations and accused persons rather than government prosecutors. This preferential consideration takes the form of a greater willingness of the Court to entertain petitions brought by common persons, even when the petitions are weak and unlikely to prevail after a full hearing. In other words, the poor and disadvantaged may not be more likely to win in the end, but they are more likely to receive a full hearing from the Supreme Court.

This is not to say that the critics of the Supreme Court have it wrong. After all, favouring the common person only at the admission stage and then rejecting their claims after a full hearing may be cold comfort to those seeking justice. And in other ways, the Supreme Court favours the rich, as we shall show in Chapter 3, which describes the influence of elite attorneys at the Supreme Court. In this chapter, we argue that the Supreme Court's way of being a 'people's court' by favouring the common person for access to *the Court* at the admission stage, does more harm than good to their interest in access to *justice*. We conclude this chapter by pointing the way toward a new vision of how the Supreme Court can more truly be a 'people's court'.

A New Twist on the Data

For years, scholars have been looking at the success rates of different parties in the Supreme Court. The theory has been that parties that are favoured by the Court will have higher win rates. For example, Professor Balakrishnan Rajagopal argues that the Court increasingly shows a tendency to decide against impoverished persons.[7] Citing cases arising after the 1990s, Professor Manoj Mate argues that the Court's rulings favour corporations and business interests when fundamental rights claims are at stake.[8] Professor Varun Gauri uses similar empirical analysis to argue that the Court increasingly disfavours disadvantaged groups.[9] All of these scholars base their conclusions on the assumption that a higher win rate for a group means that the Court is biased in favour of that group.

But what if sometimes this logic was backwards? It might sound counter-intuitive, but what if a *lower* win rate was actually the sign that the Court favoured a group? This is a view that some scholars have begun to take seriously. Professors Sudhir Krishnaswamy and Madhav Khosla have pointed out that win rates in the Supreme Court depend on which cases the Court has admitted for full hearings.[10] The Court does not give a full hearing to every case that seeks admission. It selects which cases to admit for a full hearing. As we will explain, if we take this initial admissions stage into account, different win rates for different categories of litigants actually suggest that the Court is giving preferential treatment—in some senses at least—to the group with lower win rates!

This idea has a profound impact on how we think about win rates in the Supreme Court, so we will explain it in more detail here.[11] Let's begin by recalling that more than 80 per cent of the Supreme Court's docket is devoted to SLPs.[12] The Court receives over 60,000 SLPs per year.[13] As we have described, each of these petitions receive an initial hearing which usually lasts less than two minutes. After this initial hearing, the Court decides whether to admit the petition for full proceedings or to dismiss it. (Sometimes, the Court holds more detailed hearings before making its decision on admission.) The decision to admit or dismiss a petition is a discretionary one. The Court can admit or dismiss on whatever grounds it sees fit.[14]

The Court admits about 10,000 SLPs and rejects the rest. Rejected SLPs receive nothing more from the Court. In contrast, admitted SLPs in some cases may receive a full hearing in which the parties can make all of their arguments. Afterwards, the Court renders a judgment and issues an opinion. In other cases, the Court may summarily admit and then dispose of the case without a lengthy hearing.

Thus, the decision to admit an SLP is the key choice that the Court makes in determining how much access to give a petitioner. All petitioners have a minimum amount of access—the two-minute hearing—but some parties whose petitions are admitted get much more time with the Court. If the Court wants to provide more access to a group, therefore, it will give the group preferential treatment when deciding whether to admit or reject their SLPs.

Ideally, therefore, we would want to measure whether the Court gives the common person preferential treatment when making admissions decisions. This would help answer the question whether the Court is a 'people's court', in the sense that it provides access to the common person and gives 'preferential consideration' to the poor and disadvantaged, exactly as the Court claimed in *Bihar Legal Support Society*.

How do we do this? We look for evidence that the Court sets an easier standard for admitting petitions brought by weaker parties and a stricter standard for admitting petitions brought by more powerful parties.[15] Let's say there are two cases, both involving criminal prosecutions against accused persons. We will call them Case 1 and Case 2. In these cases, the government prosecutor is the powerful party and the accused person—who is typically a less-resourced individual—is the weak party. In Case 1, the accused has been convicted, and is challenging the conviction before the Court. In Case 2, the accused has been acquitted, and the prosecution is challenging the acquittal before the Court.

In this example, one petition is brought by an accused person, while the other petition is brought by the government. If the Court gives 'preferential consideration' to the disadvantaged, it will set an easier standard for admitting the petition by the accused person who seeks to be free (Case 1), as compared to the petition by the government (Case 2).

Setting an easier standard for accused persons implies that the Court will admit even those petitions which are relatively weak, that is, which have a low chance of winning. Setting a stricter standard for the prosecution implies that petitions from the prosecution will be admitted only if their chance of success is strong. If the Court does this, this is 'preferential consideration' for the accused, who are, as a class, disadvantaged as compared to the State. Their petitions are more likely to receive a full hearing, even if they do not appear likely to succeed.

If so, then the Court will be willing to admit SLPs brought by accused persons, even if their arguments do not appear very strong. The pool of admitted appeals by accused persons will therefore contain a mix of strong and weak cases. This means that when the Court ultimately decides those cases, on average, the accused will do relatively poorly, because many of the cases are weak. These individuals will have their day in court, even if their cases are weak.

In contrast, the Court will not be willing to admit weak SLPs brought by the government but will only admit the strongest appeals. As a consequence, the Court will admit relatively fewer appeals by the government, but a larger fraction of these appeals will succeed. In short, the Court will be 'picky' with SLPs by the government.

We can learn something from looking at the win rates of different groups when their appeals are decided by the Supreme Court. But *what we learn* is surprising: When the Court provides more access to a group, it admits more weak cases, so that group has lower win rates.

If the Court is a 'people's court' and provides greater access to the disadvantaged, what will the data look like? We think that a 'people's court' will do the following:

- In civil cases between individuals and the government, giving greater access to individuals,
- In criminal cases, giving greater access to the accused rather than the State, and
- Giving greater access to cases raising constitutional challenges over cases raising other issues. This assumes that giving preferential treatment to the disadvantaged involves protecting their fundamental rights under the Constitution.

Below, we present our results from our analysis of five years of Supreme Court judgments. This research offers a new, data-driven approach that utilizes information on thousands of cases that we have collected and analysed statistically. As we will show below, we found that the Court favours individuals over the government in civil cases, the accused over the State in criminal cases, and cases involving constitutional challenges over other cases. This evidence allows us to conclude that the Court gives preferential access to groups most likely to include the disadvantaged: individuals suing the government, accused persons and constitutional claimants.

Prioritizing Access to Individuals over the Government in Civil Cases

As noted above, when a group is favoured for access, we predict that it will actually have a *lower* rate of winning at the Supreme Court as compared to other groups that appeal to the Supreme Court.

In civil cases, providing access to the disadvantaged means giving 'preferential consideration' to the poor or the common person, as opposed to large corporations or the government. In our data, we cannot distinguish between rich and poor individuals or large and small corporations, but there are two groups who we know have a power imbalance between them—individuals and the government. When a single person must take on the government, the individual is generally disadvantaged in the fight. Thus, if the Court is willing to take weak appeals from individuals, but will not take weak appeals from the government, then individuals will have a lower rate of winning when they are the party appealing against the government than when the government is the party that appeals.

In our data, this is exactly what we see. The Court admits more weak appeals brought by individuals than by the government, as shown by the lower success rates of individuals compared to the government[16]:

- Civil Appeals by individuals: Court rules in the individual's favour 53 per cent of the time
- Civil Appeals by the government: Court rules in the government's favour 69 per cent of the time

This is consistent with the idea that the Court provides greater access to individuals than the government.

Prioritizing Access to the Accused over the Government in Criminal Cases

In criminal cases, providing access to the disadvantaged means giving 'preferential consideration' to accused persons, rather than the government that is prosecuting them. So, if the Court favours the accused persons for access, it is willing to take weaker appeals from the accused persons, and we might expect to see that when the accused are the ones appealing, they win less often than when the government is the appellant.

In our data, this is exactly what we see. When the prosecution appeals to the Court, the Court rules in its favour more often than when the accused is the appellant:[17]

- Criminal Appeals by accused persons: Court rules in the accused person's favour 51 per cent of the time
- Criminal Appeals by the government: Court rules in the government's favour 59 per cent of the time

This suggests that the Court has a lower bar for admissions when an appeal is made by an accused person than by the Government. In other words, it gives more access to accused persons.

Prioritizing Access for Constitutional Cases

Next, we ask: Relative to other cases, does the Court favour constitutional cases by providing them with more access to full hearings?

Our data says that the answer is, 'Yes'. The Court does give preferential consideration to constitutional challenges arising in SLPs. In cases involving constitutional challenges, the Court rules in favour of the party appealing about 13 per cent less often than in other cases:[18]

- Constitutional challenges: Court rules in favour of the party appealing 45 per cent of the time
- All other cases: Court rules in favour of the party appealing 58 per cent of the time

This indicates that the Court may set a lower threshold for admitting constitutional cases for hearing on merits. This is also consistent with the Court's vision that it provides access to the disadvantaged. Constitutional cases are disproportionately likely to consist of challenges implicating the rights of individuals than cases that do not involve constitutional challenges. Thus, the fact that those appealing constitutional cases are more likely to lose their case than those appealing other types of cases suggests that the Court admits weaker cases when they involve constitutional issues.

In conclusion, we find that the Court's behaviour is consistent with its vision of a people's court—a court that is especially willing to hear the claims of individuals and give them greater access as compared to the government. The Court also prioritizes constitutional cases for access over non-constitutional cases.

The Broader Picture: A Lot of Hearings but Little New Law

Our analysis indicates that the Court is a people's court, in the sense that it gives preferential consideration of claims brought to it by individuals facing the government in civil cases, accused persons in criminal cases and individuals appealing cases involving constitutional claims. Note that our analysis in this chapter does not capture other ways that the Court could be a people's court. For example, one way to be a people's court is by deciding cases in a pro-consumer (rather than pro-business), pro-tenant (rather than pro-landlord), or pro-citizen (rather than pro-government) way. The Court could be a people's court in this sense, even if it admitted very few petitions from individuals. This chapter does not show that the Court is or is not a people's court in this sense. But it does show that the Court is very focused on being a people's court in terms of granting wide access to petitions brought by individuals.

This result flows from our insight that preferential consideration of petitions means that the Court will admit weaker cases brought by preferred groups. This insight is new, but it is not the only evidence that the Court is a people's court in the sense that it prioritizes giving more access to petitioners, especially disadvantaged ones.

Below, we discuss other pieces of evidence that support this conclusion. This additional evidence also shows some of the costs of the Court's focus on broad access. The Court has limited personnel and limited time—granting more hearings means less time per hearing, and hearing more cases means less time for the Court to write judgments that could guide other courts.

The Court Admits a Large Share of Cases for Full Hearings

At the most basic level, we would expect that a court that is concerned about providing access will simply admit more cases for hearings—

giving more access requires hearing more cases. Indeed, from 2010 to 2014, the Court made admissions decisions on 3,42,417 cases, which amounts to over 60,000 cases per year. Of these 3,42,417 cases, the Court admitted 47,806 cases or nearly 10,000 cases per year. In other words, the Court admitted 14 per cent (one out of every seven) of the petitions presented to it. Not only is 14 per cent a big percentage relative to other apex courts—the US Supreme Court for example admits about 1 per cent of all cases seeking admission[19]—but deciding such a huge number of cases in such a short period comes at a cost, which we explore below.

The Court Holds Huge Numbers of Hearings

The Supreme Court conducts a staggering number of hearings. While it grants full hearings to about 10,000 cases per year, this is only after it has conducted a court hearing for *every single petition* presented to it—which is more than 60,000 petitions per year. Further, each case on average involves at least two hearings.[20] Even accounting for the fact that sometimes petitions are grouped together to be resolved in a single hearing, this means that the Supreme Court holds tens of thousands, and possibly more than 1,00,000 hearings per year, every year.

How can any court—even a court with thirty-four judges, like the Supreme Court—hear such an astounding number of cases? First, the Court divides its cases among the judges, with no more than two judges sitting together for most hearings. The first hearing for admissions is before a bench of two judges, and 93 per cent of the Court's decisions, even after a case is admitted and given a full hearing, are made by two-judge benches.[21]

Second, the judges of the Court must spend most of their time in hearings. Himanshu Agarwal and Professor Rahul Hemrajani, in an innovative study of how the Court spends its time on hearings, note that the Court 'hears cases for 4.5 hours a day, 5 days a week'.[22] It devotes two days of every week (Monday and Friday) to hearings to determine whether to admit petitions, and Tuesday, Wednesday, and Thursday for full hearings on admitted cases and hearings on other matters.

Third, each hearing is very short. In their study, Hemrajani and Agarwal generated precise estimates of the time the Court spent on hearings. The most common type of case in the Supreme Court is a special leave petition (SLP). The Court hears tens of thousands of SLPs each year. And how much time does a hearing on an SLP take? The typical admission hearing lasts *less than two minutes*—to be precise, about one minute and thirty-three seconds.[23]

Most Court Opinions Neither Cite nor Announce the Law

Impressively, the Court generates nearly 1000 written and published judgments per year, averaging ten pages each in length.[24] Yet the staggering workload of the Supreme Court means that judges have precious little time to devote to writing judgments. This impairs the judges' ability to write detailed decisions that cite earlier cases, discuss how existing law applies to the current case, and announce new legal rules. In a study of thousands of Supreme Court opinions over the history of the Court, Professors Andrew Green and Albert Yoon show that many Supreme Court opinions (in some years, more than half) contain no citation to precedent.[25] Further, most judgments by the Supreme Court decide the individual case but have no effect on the law. Green and Yoon show that most decisions of the Supreme Court are never cited by subsequent decisions of the Supreme Court.[26]

This lack of legal analysis is a major cost of the Court giving access to more cases rather than announcing legal rules for courts to follow. In its decision in the *Bihar Legal Support Society* case, quoted at the beginning of this chapter, the Court said, '[T]his Court . . . was created as an apex court for the purpose of laying down the law for the entire country'.[27] But as our data shows and Professors Green and Yoon's study confirms, the Court simply does not have the time to do this when it is conducting tens of thousands of hearings per year. A judicial opinion that neither cites prior judgments nor is itself ever cited does not add to the legal rules and precedent that guide the Indian court system. Further, because the Court manages its huge caseload by dividing its strength into two-judge benches, this further limits the ability of the Court to develop consistent precedent over time. By the Supreme Court's own rules, two-judge benches lack the authority to overturn earlier precedents.

There are countless cases that could serve as examples of how the Supreme Court's opinions neither cite nor announce law. For concreteness, we will provide two examples here. One is a high-profile case involving the current chief minister of Andhra Pradesh, Y.S. Jagan Mohan Reddy, while the other is a low-profile divorce proceeding similar to thousands of others like it. Although these cases involve very different facts, we see that the Court addresses them in a similar fashion—it decides the case with attention to the facts, but it provides no analysis of legal rules or precedents, nor does it announce rules to guide future cases.

Reddy

The first case, *Y.S. Jagan Mohan Reddy v. CBI*,[28] was about granting bail in a criminal prosecution. Reddy, then a member of Parliament (MP), was accused of various offences relating to corruption. He was arrested pending completion of the investigation and trial. He sought bail from the trial court as well as the high court, but his application was rejected by both. On appeal before the Supreme Court, the only question was whether bail should be granted or not. The Court admitted the petition. In its decision, it described the charges against Reddy and the concerns raised by the investigating authority that if Reddy were out on bail, he could hamper the investigation. After describing the various charges and concerns raised, the Court's decision stated that it would not grant bail on the basis of 'all these facts and the huge magnitude of the case and also the request of the [investigating authority] asking for further time for completion of the investigation'. Notably, the entire discussion revolved only around the facts of the case. The Court did not discuss any law or cite any precedent.[29]

Gupta

The second case, *Darshan Gupta v. Radhika Gupta*,[30] was about whether or not a divorce should be granted. Darshan Gupta filed for divorce against his wife, Radhika Gupta. As grounds for divorce, he alleged that she had treated him with cruelty and was of unsound mind. The family court rejected these contentions and refused to grant divorce. The high court upheld the family court's decision. On appeal before the Supreme Court, the Court admitted the matter, and sought to reach an amicable settlement between the parties which failed. In its opinion, the Supreme Court recited the history of the case and described the evidence recorded by the lower courts. It then proceeded to give its own assessment of whether the facts made out a case for cruelty and whether Darshan Gupta had succeeded in proving that his wife was of unsound mind. In the end, without citing any law to support its interpretation of the facts, the Court decided that a divorce should not be granted.[31] This was in agreement with the lower courts, and so the Supreme Court upheld the decisions of those courts.

The Supreme Court is a People's Court—but It Serves the People in the Wrong Way

Let us now return to the question whether the Supreme Court is a people's court. One way to define 'people's court' is to say that the Court makes extra effort to give a full hearing to the poor and downtrodden. As we have shown earlier, the Court is a people's court in this sense. It lives up to its claim that it gives 'preferential consideration' to the disadvantaged.

But providing access to the disadvantaged is only one way that the Court can be a 'people's court'. And it might not be the best way. Giving common persons greater access to the Supreme Court may help those individuals who come to the Supreme Court, but what about the millions of other disadvantaged people who never come to the Supreme Court to ask for a hearing? Another way in which the Supreme Court could be a 'people's court' is by focusing its attention on *announcing the law*, so that it can give clear rules to all courts and litigants. These rules can help the disadvantaged in two ways. First, the Court can announce rules that give them greater rights. Second, by announcing clear and simple rules, the Court can make the system easier to use. This benefits all users of the Courts, but it especially benefits the poor by reducing the cost of navigating the Court system or having their case resolved in lower courts which may be located closer to them.

The Supreme Court is the only court in India that can be a people's court in this unique sense. After all, the Supreme Court is 'supreme'—it is the top court in the land, with authority to direct the decision-making of all other courts.[32] Because the Supreme Court sits at the very top of the Indian court system, it alone has the power to announce the rules for all other courts to follow. In this role, the Court could focus its attention on hearing petitions and appeals that raise legal questions that need clarification. In these cases, the Court could explain how the Constitution and statutes apply in different factual situations. It could interpret ambiguous or vague language in statutes to clarify their meaning. And, it could create and announce new rules when existing laws do not address a problem.

In many cases over the years, it has issued many famous judgments that announce important principles or new rules that apply to all of India, not just to the parties in those cases. But in recent decades, announcing the law has become a small part of the overall work of the Court. Most of its time is consumed with sifting through over 60,000 SLPs per year, admitting around 10,000 cases for hearing each year, and deciding countless cases that do not announce any law—cases like *Reddy* and *Gupta*.

Providing clear, authoritative guidance to the courts of India requires the Supreme Court to devote significant time to each case that it hears, so that it can write a detailed judgment that explains and announces the rules for other courts to follow. To perform this role effectively, therefore, the Supreme Court must hear relatively few cases. The Supreme Court is not a 'people's court' in this sense of the term.

Conclusion: Rethinking What It Means to Be a People's Court

In this chapter, we have considered the question of whether the Supreme Court is a 'people's court' and, more importantly, whether that is a good thing. The Court has been criticized for not being a 'people's court', because disadvantaged groups do not win as often in the Court as other groups.

As we've shown in this chapter, though, this claim is mistaken. The Court chooses which petitions to admit and which to dismiss, and the Court selectively favours petitions from the disadvantaged—individuals versus the government, accused persons versus criminal prosecutors, people bringing claims for constitutional rights—even when their petitions make weak claims. This means that preferential access for a group leads to that group having lower win rates in the Supreme Court—a surprising but important insight.

But there is a deeper question here. Even if the Court provides more access to the disadvantaged, is that a good thing? Or is there a better way for the Court to protect the interests of disadvantaged groups? As we have explained in this chapter, the wide access that the Court provides does not come for free. Its unending stream of hearings leaves its judges with precious little time to focus their attention on cases of greater significance to the law. Further, the constant crush of cases leads to long delays in the Court and overworked judges. We discuss the implications of such delays in Chapter 2.

We are of the view that although the Court is a 'people's court', it may not be the right kind of 'people's court'. Today, it is a 'people's court' by *providing access* to tens of thousands of petitioners every year and by holding tens of thousands of hearings per year. This is an amazing feat and is part of what makes the Court popular and admired in India and internationally. But the Court's single-minded focus on maximizing access may be doing more harm than good. It could be a court for the people in a very different way—by focusing on *announcing the law*. We therefore conclude this chapter with four key observations that highlight the costs of the Court's focus on access and the possibility of a better alternative.

Our key ideas are these:

- The Supreme Court approach of admitting a large number of cases has backfired, because the huge caseload causes long delays, which are costly for the poor and disadvantaged.

- The Court can affect more cases involving the poor and disadvantaged by announcing rules for lower courts to follow, rather than by deciding cases one-by-one.
- Even if disadvantaged groups have less access to the Supreme Court, announcing clear rules will provide them with more access to the lower courts.
- Broad access is a choice the Court has made and a choice the Court can change if it is determined to do so.

In the sections below, we elaborate on each one of these four ideas. Ultimately, we conclude that the problem is not that the Court fails to make access to the disadvantaged a priority but that the Court defines 'access to justice' too narrowly. It focuses on access to the Supreme Court, without considering how its decisions could affect access to justice in all of the other courts in India. A smaller caseload in the Supreme Court, with fewer hearings, would permit a focus on forming larger benches to deliberate longer on cases and write opinions that give clarity to the law and direction to the lower courts. Such an approach would provide benefits to the millions of poor and disadvantaged litigants in India who never reach the Supreme Court.

Access Causes Delay

In the abstract, giving more access to the Court seems like a good thing. Every time the Court admits a petition for a full hearing, it is another opportunity to do justice for someone who might have a legitimate argument that the lower courts caused an injustice. But in reality, giving more access has many effects, not all of them positive. The most obvious effect is delay.

It is well known that cases can take decades to resolve within the Indian judicial system. Decrying this phenomenon, human rights advocates invoke the refrain that 'justice delayed is justice denied'. Economists and businesspersons have also raised the alarm on delays because they believe lengthy case disposition times inhibit investment by foreign companies and have other negative impacts on economic growth.[33]

What is less well known is that delay is not just a problem for the lower courts of India but a serious problem in the Supreme Court too. Our dataset of Supreme Court judgments gives insight into exactly how serious this problem is. We find that the average time from the date of decision by the Court below to the date of decision by the Supreme Court is 1542 days.[34] This is more than four years and two months! (Notably, based on our data, the Supreme Court is not any faster than the trial courts or the high courts. We discuss the problem of delay in more detail in Chapter 2.) Worse, this is the time taken for the cases that have been decided; it does not account for the thousands more cases still pending in the system awaiting decision.

The Court's extreme commitment to providing access is a cause of these long backlogs. Providing more access means a heavier caseload for the Court, which in turn causes delays.

Delays hurt everyone who seeks resolution of their case, but not everyone suffers equally. What is easy to overlook is that delay hurts the poor and disadvantaged more. The simple reality is that rich litigants who claim to be owed money can afford to wait and poor litigants cannot. Rich litigants accused of crimes can afford to pay bail while their appeal drags on and poor litigants cannot. Rich litigants might be able to speed up their cases by hiring expensive and sophisticated lawyers while litigants from disadvantaged groups are not likely to have the same resources.

Changing the focus of the Court away from providing access would mean the Court would admit fewer cases. The cases that remain would be resolved sooner. Justice accelerated would be justice improved.

A Drop in the Ocean

Holding tens of thousands of hearings per year is a testament to the work ethic of the judges of the Supreme Court. It is also a testament to a desire to give a hearing to every person, rich or poor, who comes to the Court. But the strategy of helping the poor and oppressed by deciding individual cases one at a time is a doomed strategy. No matter how liberally the Court grants hearings, it can never reach more than a tiny fraction of all of the poor in the Indian court system.

The Supreme Court issues about 1000 judgments per year. Some of these judgments resolve more than one case, so each year the Court resolves more than 1000 cases after full hearings. This is a big number of cases and many of these cases involve the poor and disadvantaged.

In comparison, though, India is the second-largest country in the world by population, with more than 1.4 billion people. Its court system is the largest court system in a democracy in the world, with literally millions of cases each year. Even if one looks only at the high courts, which hear a small fraction of the cases in the Indian court system, they decide 1.2 million cases per year.

What is 1000 compared to 1.2 million? It is not even 'a drop in a bucket'. It is more like a drop in the ocean. For every poor person who has a hearing in the Supreme Court, there may be 1000 others in the high courts, and 10,000 others in other courts, who receive no benefit from the Supreme Court at all.

They receive no benefit from the Court because most of the Court's decisions do little to provide guidance to the high courts and the other lower courts. Judicial opinions like *Reddy* and *Gupta* don't give rules or instructions for other courts to follow. By giving access to the 10,000 cases it admits each year, the Court is giving nothing to the 1.2 million cases in the high courts that it never sees nor provides any guidance to.

Indeed, the effect on litigants in the lower courts may be worse than nothing. Two scholars of the Court, Rishad Chowdhury and Nick Robinson, have argued that the huge numbers of opinions issued by the Court every year not only fail to benefit litigants in the lower court, but may even make them worse off. The thousands of opinions that neither cite legal precedent nor announce rules send unclear and sometimes contradictory signals to the lower courts on how to decide cases. Confusion about legal rules leads to more errors in the lower courts and because the vast majority of cases in the lower courts never reach the Supreme Court, these errors go uncorrected.[35]

Access to Justice, not Access to the Supreme Court

It is essential to distinguish the broader concept of 'access to justice' from the narrower concept of 'access to the Supreme Court'. There is no question that access to justice for the common person, the poor and the disadvantaged is an important goal of any court, including the Supreme Court of India.

For nearly all of the 1.4 billion people in India, access to justice means access to trial courts, administrative tribunals and maybe the high courts. It does not mean access to the Supreme Court. As we have noted, of the millions of cases filed in the Indian courts every year, only about 10,000 ever end up being given a detailed hearing by the Supreme Court.

This means that improving access to justice requires making it easier for the poor and disadvantaged to get a hearing in one of the thousands of lower courts and administrative tribunals that hear millions of cases each year. The best way to improve access to justice may be for the Court to announce clear legal rules that let the disadvantaged know what their rights are in the lower courts.

The Court's Huge Caseload is Not Inevitable

The Supreme Court has a huge caseload and the number of petitions filed with the Court has been rising over time. This will not change any time soon. But the Court can control how many and what kind of petitions it admits. As we have noted, whether to admit or dismiss a petition is entirely within the discretion of the Court. One change that the Court could make is simply to admit fewer cases. The Court does not need to admit 10,000 cases for full hearings every year. By changing its approach to admitting petitions, it could immediately reduce the burden of holding thousands of hearings every month. Abhinav Chandrachud has noted, however, that one of the reasons the Supreme Court has not reduced its SLP petitions admissions rates is because of the resistance by the lawyers who practice before it. Those lawyers have a lot to lose if the Court took fewer cases.[36]

Another change the Court could make is to choose its cases differently. Currently, as cases like *Reddy* and *Gupta* illustrate, the Court admits most cases to decide them on their individual facts. This merely duplicates the work of the lower courts. Instead, the Court could look for cases that raise important or difficult questions of law. By answering these questions, the Court could give clear guidance to the lower courts on how *they* should decide the millions of cases they must decide.

Currently, the norm of the Court is to admit lots of petitions, with no special focus on cases with important legal questions. In early 2016, a Constitution Bench of the Supreme Court had the opportunity to announce guidelines for how the Court would admit or dismiss petitions, but it declined to do so.[37]

This reluctance to set guidelines has never been the universal view of the judges of the Court. In the *Bihar Legal* decision itself, the Court took the view that petitions that are admitted 'would be exceptional by their very nature' and that the Court should not interfere in every case where 'some injustice has been done'.[38] And in our off-the-record conversations with judges of the Court, judges have expressed views of this nature too. In conversation, one judge noted that so much of the litigation before the Supreme Court involves routine disputes over case-specific facts. He then asked rhetorically, 'Why are these cases going to the Supreme Court?'

In our view, this is exactly the question the Court should be asking itself.

2

Explosion, Exclusion, Evasion: The Burden of Backlogs

A Backlogged Court

The Indian judicial system is infamous for its lengthy delays in deciding cases. The National Judicial Data Grid records that in the trial courts, of the 32.5 million cases that are pending across the country, 8.6 per cent, or roughly one in eleven cases, has been pending for more than ten years at only the trial court level.[1] At the high court level, of the 4.8 million cases currently on the courts' dockets, 19 per cent or approximately one in five cases, was filed more than ten years ago in the high court.[2] Nearly 15 per cent of writ petitions for the enforcement of fundamental rights, or the performance of public functions or statutory or public duties,[3] have been pending in the high courts for more than ten years.[4]

The National Judicial Data Grid does not provide data for the Supreme Court, perhaps a reflection of the fact that in judicial policy-making circles, delay is often seen as a lower court problem.[5] Other studies indicate that in 2011, 17 per cent of the cases on the Supreme Court's regular hearing docket had been pending for more than five years, up from 7 per cent in 2004.[6] Our study, based on scraping data of all cases from the Supreme Court of India website, finds that as of

November 2018, a whopping 39.57 per cent of cases in the Supreme Court were pending for more than five years, and an *additional* 7.74 per cent cases were pending for more than ten years. Of the disposed cases,[7] the median disposal time (that is, the disposal time for half the cases) is within approximately one and a half years from filing. However, the average time that the Court takes for disposal is approximately two and a half years. By itself, this might not sound like a long time. But if half the cases are taking less than a year and a half, and the average case is taking two and a half years, this implies that at the top end, the time elapsed in disposing cases is very high, thus pulling up the average. This can be seen from the fact that the fastest one-fifths (20th percentile) of the cases took up to eighty-nine days (or around three months) from filing to disposal after admission, whereas the slowest one-fifths (the 80th percentile) took four years and four months or longer from filing to disposal.[8] The slowest of cases, at the 95th percentile, took eight years and three months or longer to disposal. Overall then, the Supreme Court appears to provide two track justice—super-fast disposals for some cases and long gestation periods for others.

The average time lapse between filing and disposal of cases at the Supreme Court is comparable to that of trial courts and the high courts. Cases that make it all the way from the trial court to the Supreme Court take, on average, around thirteen years and six months from first entering the judicial system to disposal by the Supreme Court.[9] The Supreme Court itself accounts for about one-third of this total, approximately on a par with the average amount of time taken at each tier of the judiciary.[10]

Time Lapse in Disposal by Type of Case and Subject Matter

Our data on the Supreme Court reveals that writ petitions take on average around one and a half years for disposal, appeals take around three years and SLP admissions matters where notice is issued to the other side but leave is ultimately denied, take around two years for disposal.

Case Type	Number of days between filing and disposal dates	Number of cases in our data
Writ Petition (Civil)	418	105
Writ Petition (Criminal)	537	34
Civil Appeal	1322	1,23,171
Criminal Appeal	1190	22,856
Special Leave Petition (Civil)	860	2,62,644
Special Leave Petition (Criminal)	678	55,687

Table 1: The time lapse between filing and disposal of different types of cases at the Supreme Court

The Supreme Court registry classifies cases under forty-four subject matter heads. Our data on the time lapse in disposal of cases by subject matter is quite revealing. The top three categories in terms of time lapse between filing and disposal are seven-judge, nine-judge and five-judge bench matters respectively, ranging from five to nine years for disposal on average. Benches of these sizes decide the most contentious issues before the Supreme Court. The Constitution requires that all cases involving a substantial question of law as to the interpretation of the Constitution should be decided by benches of five or more judges.[11]

Indirect tax and state excise matters are also high on the list of cases with the greatest time lapse. These cases impact the exchequer as well as the conduct of business, but take on average around four years to decide in the Supreme Court. Land laws, agricultural tenancies and eviction matters take on average around three years at the Supreme Court, as do service matters relating to public employment.

Case Subject Matter (Top ten by average duration)	Number of days between filing and disposal dates	Number of observations
Seven-Judges Bench Matter	3304	13
Nine-Judges Bench Matter	2886	3760
Five-Judges Bench Matter	1808	789
Three-Judges Bench Matter	1568	4604

Case Subject Matter (Top ten by average duration)	Number of days between filing and disposal dates	Number of observations
Indirect Taxes Matters	1567	17,006
State Excise-Trading in Liquor-Privileges, Licences-Distilleries and Breweries	1356	2324
Matters Relating to Judiciary	1203	1314
Land Laws and Agricultural Tenancies	1149	13,089
Eviction under the Public Premises (Eviction) Act	1140	852
Service Matters	1115	48,990

Table 2: Time lapse between filing and disposal by subject matter of cases.

These are cases that have been disposed of. Our data on cases that are pending in the Court paint an even more disturbing picture. As of November 2018, the Constitution Bench matters that had not been disposed of had been pending for more than eight and a half years on average, going up to 16.3 years on average for seven-judge bench matters. Matters relating to land laws, educational matters, money matters and disturbingly, criminal matters and family law matters, were pending on average for over six and a half years. The subject category that had been on the docket for the shortest average time was habeas corpus petitions. However, even this 'great writ of liberty' had been pending on average for two and a half years, with half the matters pending for more than two years.

Case Subject Matter	Days pending since being filed in SC	No. of cases
Seven-Judges Bench	5822	103
Nine-Judges Bench Matter	4393	296
Five-Judges Bench Matter	3044	359
Matters Relating to Commissions of Enquiry	3002	20

Case Subject Matter	Days pending since being filed in SC	No. of cases
Appointments etc. of constitutional Functionaries	2929	15
Three-Judges Bench Matter	2924	1981
Land Laws and Agricultural Tenancies	2714	4058
Admission to Educational Institutions other than Medical and Engineering	2685	223
Allocation of 15 per cent All India Quota in Admission/Transfer to Medical Colleges	2615	2
Admiralty and Maritime Laws	2538	30
Admission/Transfer to Engineering and Medical Colleges	2514	1337
Simple Money and Mortgage Matters etc.	2427	307
Mines, Minerals and Mining Leases	2398	1433
Criminal Matters	2223	25,194
Family Law Matters	2215	3070
Matters Pertaining to Armed Forces & Para Military Forces	2210	1049
Letter Petition and PIL Matters	2157	2249
State Excise-Trading in Liquor-Privileges, Licences-Distilleries Breweries	2141	884
Ordinary Civil Matters	2128	19,958
Rent Act Matters	2119	1061
Labour Matters	2070	4928
Company Law, MRTP and Allied Matters	2035	2601
Matters Relating to Judiciary	1938	553
Mercantile Laws, Commercial Transactions including Banking	1888	1151
Indirect Taxes Matters	1887	18,948
Religious and Charitable Endowments	1879	1641
Establishment and Recognition of Educational Institutions	1845	256
Direct Taxes Matters	1843	11.256

Case Subject Matter	Days pending since being filed in SC	No. of cases
Arbitration Matters	1784	2282
Election Matters	1726	761
Matters Relating to Leases, Govt. Contracts and Contracts by Local Bodies	1716	460
Matters Relating to Consumer Protection	1689	3935
Service Matters	1688	19,749
Contempt of Court Matters	1489	711
Land Acquisition and Requisition Matters	1454	13,162
Statutory Appointments	1444	41
Eviction under the Public Premises (Eviction) Act	1393	158
Academic Matters	1371	178
Compensation Matters	1205	1308
Appeal Against Orders of Statutory Bodies	1132	1395
Other	1108	3
Defective Matter as not re-filed	911	267
Habeas Corpus Matters	896	22

Table 3: Length of case pendency in the Supreme Court by subject matter

Causes and Consequences of Delay

Docket Explosion and Strained Resources

Why do cases take so long to decide in the Supreme Court? The causes are many. One reason is docket explosion—the Court today receives around 60,000 appeals and petitions each year. Compare this to the approximately 35,000 cases filed at the Court twenty years ago or the approximately 20,000 cases filed around 1980.[12] The bulk of these cases are appeals from the orders of lower courts and tribunals, under the Court's SLP jurisdiction. SLPs, which used to comprise around 82 per cent of the Court's admissions docket in 1993, rose to around 85 per cent of the docket by 2011. As of March 2018, appeals, the bulk of them SLPs, comprised approximately 99 per cent of the Court's docket of pending cases (including cases pending admission),[13] and about 88 per cent of its docket of admitted and disposed matters.[14]

The burgeoning SLP docket comprising primarily appeals in civil and criminal cases has crowded out writ petitions and constitutional challenges. By 2011, writ petitions filed directly in the Supreme Court comprised only around 2 per cent of the admissions docket;[15] by 2016, they accounted for about 8 per cent of the Court's admitted and disposed cases.[16] Constitutional matters also form a very small part of the cases admitted through the SLP route—less than 4 per cent.[17] PILs, which are often the most high-profile component of the Court's docket, comprise only about 0.6 per cent of the Court's case load[18] and form only 3 per cent of the reported judgments of the Court.[19] Even though such cases often deal with some of the most pressing problems facing large parts of the country, they take on average around three years from filing to disposal.[20]

As we have noted before, because the volume of special leave petitions is so high, judges spend very little time—on average only ninety-three seconds per matter,[21] to decide whether to admit the case or not. Most matters are dismissed outright on the very first hearing. Between 2015 and 2019, both inclusive, the Court rejected roughly seven out of every eight cases in which it decided on the admission application.[22] If the Court is inclined to admit the matter, it typically issues notice to the other party—the respondent—to appear and argue why the case should not be admitted.[23] In recent times, this 'after notice' stage has become a substantive intermediate step between admissions and hearing on merits. After hearing both parties, the Court may dispose of the case by refusing to admit the matter, or by admitting the matter and posting it for a detailed hearing on merits, or by issuing a ruling on merits based on the arguments made by the parties at the admissions stage. Some of these 'after notice' or 'final disposal' matters are listed on Mondays and Fridays, but increasingly also on the 'regular hearing days' of Tuesdays, Wednesdays and Thursdays.[24] Thus, a large part of the Court's workweek is spent deciding which new cases to admit, rather than hearing the cases that are already admitted. This too adds to the delay in disposing 'after notice' and admitted cases.

In battling the huge volume of cases coming before it, the Court has taken two steps to increase available judicial resources. First, the composition of the Supreme Court has increased dramatically over the years—from eight judges in 1950 to thirty-four at present. Secondly, judges increasingly sit in smaller benches—87 per cent of all cases decided by the Court between 2010 and 2015 were before two-judge benches; almost all others were before three-judge benches. Less than 1 per cent of cases before the Court were before Constitution Benches (of five or more judges). As we have noted above, Constitution Benches take anywhere between five to nine years on average to decide cases, which is partly a function of the Court's inability to spare enough judges to constitute large benches. Larger benches have declined in frequency—from an average of seventy-one per year in the first twenty-five years of the Constitution to only eleven per year in the next twenty-five.[25] Though the Constitution requires that substantial questions as to the interpretation of the Constitution be decided by Constitution Benches, we find that in the period between 2010 and 2015, two-judge benches decided 78 per cent of the constitutional challenges before the Court.[26] This includes significant constitutional cases which determined important questions of constitutional law such as *Suresh Kumar Koushal v. Naz Foundation*,[27] where in 2013, the Supreme Court upheld the constitutionality of Section 377, Indian Penal Code, which criminalized sodomy. In September 2019, the Court further lowered its bench strength and allowed certain category of cases to be heard by judges sitting singly.[28]

Both these measures have ended up fragmenting the Court. Each bench speaks for the Court as a whole but because of the divided bench structure, benches may come in conflict or speak in different voices. This 'poly-vocality' itself becomes a source of further litigation before the courts.[29] The litigation surrounding Section 24 of the LARR Act, discussed in the Introduction, is but one example of the contestations that arise as a result of this polyvocal nature of the Indian Supreme Court.

The Expansive SLP Jurisdiction

While a significant reason for delay in the Supreme Court is the lack of adequate judicial resources to deal with the volume of cases coming in, it would be incorrect to reduce the problem of delays to only a problem of adequate resources. The Court is in many ways responsible for its own troubles. For example, the SLP jurisdiction under Article 136 was considered by the Constitution framers and by the early Court to be exceptional in nature,[30] to be used sparingly and only for admitting cases involving either 'substantial and grave injustice' of sufficient gravity to warrant a review,[31] or questions of law of general public importance.[32] However, over time, the Court has interpreted its SLP jurisdiction very widely, stating that it has the power to interfere 'even with findings of fact . . . [as for example when] the acquittal is based on an irrelevant ground, or where the High Court allows itself to be deflected by red herrings drawn across the track, or where the evidence accepted by the trial court is rejected by the High Court after a perfunctory consideration, or where the baneful approach of the High Court has resulted in vital and crucial evidence being ignored, or for any such adequate reason . . .'[33]

It is this liberal approach to SLPs that has led to the burgeoning court docket and its associated problems. However, the Court has resisted attempts to bring some structure and control to the SLP jurisdiction. A reference to a five-judge bench to decide this issue[34] failed when the Court held in 2016 that 'no effort should be made to restrict the powers of this Court under Article 136 because while exercising its powers under Article 136 of the Constitution of India, this Court can, after considering facts of the case to be decided, very well use its discretion.'[35]

As a result, there is no clear benchmark for determining which types of cases deserve admission under the SLP route. The matter has been left to the discretion, often bordering on whim, of each bench. As noted in Chapter 1, many cases before the Supreme Court under the SLP route raise no question of law at all. A study by Andrew Green and Albert Yoon found that for most of its history, about half of the Court's judgments contained no reference to prior case law. Unsurprisingly then, 60 per cent of the judgments delivered by the Court since the 1990s were never cited again in a ten-year period following the judgment.[36] Cases that neither reference any prior law, nor are cited again, likely do not touch upon any question of law at all, let alone one of general public importance.

An argument often advanced in support of an expansive SLP jurisdiction is that the Supreme Court needs to take on these cases to correct erroneous decisions by lower courts, and that the justice needs of individual litigants trumps other considerations with respect to the Court's functioning. Such an argument presumes that (a) the lower courts are severely malfunctioning, and a wide SLP jurisdiction allows the Supreme Court to 'police' these courts,[37] (b) that the Supreme Court needs to step in often to correct wrongful decisions by the lower courts[38] and (c) when the Supreme Court reverses a decision by a lower court, it is because the Supreme Court, and not the lower court, has reached the right or just conclusion. Each of these propositions is debatable.

First, the bulk of the appeals filed before the Supreme Court are not found worthy of admission—close to 88 per cent of all cases filed before the Court are dismissed at the admissions stage. Of the remaining 12 per cent of cases, the Supreme Court reverses only about 57 per cent cases.[39] This implies that for every 100 cases appealed to the Supreme Court, the Supreme Court ultimately changes the lower court decision in less than seven cases—hardly evidence of wide-spread malfunctioning.

It may be that the lower courts indeed need a lot of appellate supervision, but the most egregious wrongful decisions by lower courts are not making their way to the Supreme Court. If that is indeed the case, then this too calls for the Court to rethink its SLP admission standards. A very low threshold for admission of SLPs inevitably crowds out those who cannot afford to secure their rights by spending lots of time and resources in fighting their cases in court. The Supreme Court has itself recognized that delay in litigation 'is a great advantage for that litigant who has the longer purse'.[40]

Even in cases where the Supreme Court reverses the decision of a lower court, it is important to remember Justice Robert Jackson's warning in the context of the US Supreme Court that '[w]e are not final because we are infallible, but we are infallible only because we are final'. Just because the Supreme Court is the court of last resort—the final court of appeal—does not mean that its decisions are necessarily right.

Taken together then, by the Supreme Court's own data, there is no evidence of such systemic malfunctioning in the lower courts to require the exercise of expansive appellate supervision of such courts. Even if there is basis for the Court's distrust of lower courts, it is likely that many of the most deserving cases for the Court's intervention are crowded out due to the Court's inability to decide cases in a timely manner.

A heavily backlogged Court docket, with no clear guidance on what types of cases should be admitted, also allows for litigators and litigants to game the system, or at least to 'take a chance' on an appeal.[41] In an SLP case, the goal is to get the Court to issue notice to the other party and to stay the order or judgment that is being appealed. Our data shows that once notice is issued to the other side, a case that is ultimately disallowed takes on average around two years for disposal.[42] In addition, the Court rarely imposes costs for agitating a weak or frivolous case before the Court. In nine out of ten cases, parties are directed to bear their own costs.[43] Taken together, for a well-resourced party who has lost in the lower court, it makes strategic sense to appeal to the Supreme Court, since there is a chance that despite having a weak case, the Supreme Court may admit the matter. If the matter does get admitted, that litigant can delay legal liability for a significant amount of time and may perhaps even stretch the resources of the other side enough that they give up their claim. Even if the other side persists and wins in the Supreme Court, the Court is very unlikely to impose costs on the appellant. Thus, the Court's uncertain SLP jurisprudence and its backlog perversely attract more litigation and create a vicious cycle of delay.

Delays and the Problem of (Not) Prioritizing Cases

Due to the vast backlog, the Court has to prioritize certain cases, or certain types of cases for hearing. The power to determine 'listing' priorities—which types of cases should be taken up by the Court on priority—is invested in the Chief Justice, as part of the Master of the Roster powers. In a study of the Court's listing practices, Jahnavi Sindhu and Vikram Aditya Narayan have found that the determination of these priorities varies widely depending on the Chief Justice.[44] Since Chief Justices do not have long tenures, the listing priorities change frequently, thus adding to uncertainty about the resolution of cases pending before the Supreme Court.

Investing listing powers in the Chief Justice's sole, non-reviewable domain also raises concerns regarding the undue concentration of powers in the hands of one person, an issue we discuss in greater detail in Chapter 4. This is especially true when the Chief Justice exercises his Master of the Roster powers to list individual cases out of turn.

Individual cases can be prioritized for listing for admissions or for hearing. Lawyers can 'mention' a case before the Chief Justice and ask for the case to jump the queue and be listed for admissions hearing on priority. Every morning, the Chief Justice's court starts off with a round of 'mentioning' by lawyers seeking early listing of their cases for admissions hearings.

Early listing applications are also common for admitted matters. Once a matter has been admitted for regular hearing, even seasoned lawyers have no clarity on when the case is likely to come up for hearing on its own. An admitted matter can go for years without being assigned to a particular bench for hearing. As an Advocate-on-Record before the Supreme Court evocatively told us, 'The case disappears into a void, with little clarity on when it might re-surface.' Lawyers have two options—either wait for the matter to come up on its own in due course or file an application for early listing of the matter. If the case has not been assigned to any bench, the early hearing application is filed before the Chief Justice. If a bench has been assigned, the application goes before that bench.

While lawyers have to provide reasons for why their case deserves to jump the queue, given the huge backlogs and the large number of cases requiring out of turn hearing, this is another place where the 'face value' of the lawyer becomes important. In sum, the backlog of cases leads to uncertainty regarding listing, which is compounded by frequent queue jumping. Allegations of corruption by the registry in listing practices—listing some cases out of turn and burying others—are often made. Even the Chief Justice of India has expressed frustration in open court regarding the manner in which cases are listed by the registry.[45]

The 'pick and choose' model, through which some cases get to jump the queue and be listed for early hearing, also raises questions about the Court's institutional priorities. For example, on 6 July 2020, the Supreme Court dismissed with costs a writ against the registry for giving priority to a bail application of a prominent journalist, while the petitioner's own cases were not given adequate priority.[46] In dismissing the case, the Supreme Court observed that the case of the journalist, Arnab Goswami, was listed within hours of its being filed since '[i]t pertained to liberty and freedom of media'.[47] This statement immediately gave rise to comparisons with a contempt petition filed against the Union Territory of Jammu and Kashmir for not setting up a Supreme Court-directed mechanism to review decisions regarding internet restrictions in Jammu and Kashmir—a case which clearly pertained to the 'liberty and freedom of media' of millions of citizens. This contempt petition was filed on 8 June 2020, but was not listed for even one hearing until more than a month after it was filed.[48]

The heavy backlog in the Supreme Court has also allowed the Court to avoid difficult cases by the simple expedient of not deciding such cases at all. Court watchers have been increasingly concerned with this form of 'judicial evasion' where the Court leaves important cases hanging, while it focuses on more mundane matters.[49] For example, the Supreme Court took five years, without issuing a stay, to decide the challenge to the government's universal biometric identification scheme, AADHAAR, by which time, it had more than a billion enrollees, thus rendering the challenge virtually ineffective.[50]

Another egregious example is the *Electoral Bonds* case. In February 2018, the State promulgated an electoral bonds scheme which allows persons to purchase bonds from the State Bank of India and donate these anonymously to political parties. Through amendments to various statutes, the State sought to ensure anonymity of the donor, eliminate requirements for political parties to report the source or volume of funds gathered through electoral bonds, and remove limits on electoral financing by corporate entities. The government claimed that the purchase of bonds from authorized banks would ensure that un-taxed wealth or 'black money' is not used for campaign funding. At the same time, the anonymity in funding would protect donors from being targeted for their donations by rival political parties.

A writ petition was immediately filed before the Supreme Court against the electoral bond scheme and associated statutory amendments. Petitioners who challenged the scheme as well as the Election Commission of India objected to the scheme for shielding the sources of funding of political parties from public scrutiny, thus denying voters information that might be crucial for their voting decisions. They argued that the anonymity and the lifting of caps on funding would provide undue power to corporate interests in the governance of the country, and could also open the doors for foreign funding of political parties.

The Court issued notice to the State in the matter and posted it for a more detailed hearing, without issuing a stay in the matter. Then, the case went into the void for a year. It resurfaced in February 2019, when the petitioners mentioned the case before the Chief Justice and sought an early hearing. The matter was listed for March 2019 and ultimately heard in April 2019, just as the general elections of 2019 kicked off. The issue at stake touches on the very nature of India's democratic polity and its possible subversion. The Court itself recognized that 'the rival contentions give rise to weighty issues which have a tremendous bearing on the sanctity of the electoral process in the country.'[51] However, the Court again refused to stay the electoral bond scheme, stating instead that the matter required a detailed hearing. The general elections came and went, as did other state elections. More than three years later, as of June 2022, the Court has not found the time to hear the matter, though in the meantime, it has refused to stay the operation of the electoral bonds scheme.[52]

Important matters of the kinds discussed here often require setting up larger benches. The Chief Justice of India, as the Master of the Roster, has the power to constitute these benches.[53] The Chief Justice can exercise what is effectively a pocket-veto on the matter, by simply refusing to set up a bench in a time-appropriate manner. One easy justification for such 'evasion' is that setting up larger benches places significant burdens on the already stretched judicial resources of the Court and contributes to delays in disposing of cases across the board.[54] In effect, backlogs and delays provide easy cover, not only for greater centralization of powers in the hands of the Chief Justice, but also for the Court to evade its constitutional responsibilities.

Addressing the Problem of Backlog

Rethinking the Court's SLP jurisdiction

Overall then, the backlog of cases in the Supreme Court crowds out important cases and likely has a disparate impact on the most vulnerable litigants. The large volume of cases breaks up the jurisprudential cohesiveness of the Court and weakens the system of precedents, which in turn gives rise to more litigation. Delay in decision-making creates perverse incentives for lawyers and litigants to keep approaching the Supreme Court, to take a chance and often game the system. The press of cases not only delays decision-making but also adds to the uncertainty regarding how long the case is likely to take. This increases the power of the Chief Justice as the Master of the Roster and allows judges to evade making difficult decisions of constitutional importance.

What then can be done to reduce the backlog of cases in the Supreme Court? There is no single 'magic bullet' solution. First, of course, this is a resource problem—too many cases and too few judges. The Court has already tried increasing the number of judges. It is time to seriously consider decreasing the number of cases. Very often, decreasing the number of cases that a court takes on is seen as an impediment to access to justice. In a limitless world, this argument might have held water. However, in a system with limited resources, access to justice depends on how those resources are allocated. Trade-offs will have to be made between the quantity and quality of cases that the Court takes if it is to provide timely access to justice.

There is also a false equivalence in this argument between access to justice and access to the Supreme Court for each appeal. As we have seen in Chapter 1, the Supreme Court will provide for qualitatively better access to justice if it takes fewer cases. How might this be accomplished? For one, the Court should revisit its 2016 decision that refused to lay down clear norms and guidelines on when to exercise its SLP jurisdiction. It should take seriously, the view expressed by a two-judge bench of the Court, echoing the views of K.K. Venugopal, former Attorney General for India, that the burgeoning SLP docket has reduced the Supreme Court to an 'ordinary forum of appeal'.[55] The two-judge bench of the Court was of the view that '[u]nder the constitutional scheme, ordinarily the last court in the country in ordinary cases was meant to be the High Court. The Supreme Court as the Apex Court in the country was meant to deal with important issues like constitutional questions, questions of law of general importance or where grave injustice had been done.'[56] This bench recognized that given its limited resources, if the Supreme Court were to entertain 'all and sundry kinds of cases it will soon be flooded with a huge amount of backlog and will not be able to deal with important questions relating to the Constitution or the law or where grave injustice has been done, for which it was really meant under the constitutional Scheme'.[57] This is precisely our finding. Unfortunately, in 2016, the five-judge bench that was set up to look into this matter, decided to leave the issue of exercise of discretion in this matter to each individual judge,[58] making the circular argument that 'no effort should be made to restrict the powers of this Court under Article 136 because while exercising its powers under Article 136 of the Constitution of India, this Court can, after considering facts of the case to be decided, very well use its discretion'.[59]

However, even if the Court sets up strict norms to regulate the SLP jurisdiction, it will ultimately be left to the judgment of each bench whether a case before it fits within the norms or not. Norms will not reduce the backlog without a clear understanding within the Supreme Court that the Article 136 power is truly exceptional, and that matters should usually rest with high courts. As we have seen in this chapter, the common belief that a broad SLP jurisdiction is needed to exercise close supervision over severely malfunctioning lower courts is not borne out from the data.

Apart from admitting only the most serious cases that raise constitutional issues, or important questions of general importance, or to resolve conflicting precedents, etc., the Court can also be strategic in determining which types of cases to prioritize. For example, our data shows that in 64 per cent of the SLPs admitted by the Supreme Court between 2010 and 2015, all the lower Courts were unanimous on the outcome of the case. Where the lower courts were in agreement, the Supreme Court was 17 per cent more likely to uphold the lower court decision than if the lower courts had disagreed. This statistic can be used for a general rule of thumb—if the lower courts are unanimous on the outcome of a case, the Supreme Court should typically not admit such a matter unless the appellant makes a very compelling case for why all the lower courts got it wrong.

With time, if the Supreme Court signals that it will not easily entertain SLPs, fewer litigants are likely to waste resources on appealing in the face of near certainty of a loss. And lesser conflict of precedent may also improve decision-making by lower courts to further reduce the need for error correction by the Supreme Court.

This is easier said than done. It would be naïve to not acknowledge that perhaps the biggest impediment to any change of the sort proposed here is the Supreme Court bar, which depends on the Court's liberal filing policy for its bread and butter. These are entrenched interests and it will require strong leadership from the Court, especially the Chief Justice of India, to see reforms of this nature through.[60] Nonetheless, there are some opportunities present for incremental change that can allow the Court to begin shifting away from the current patterns of perverse incentives for lawyers to file cases.

Rethinking the Emphasis on Oral Advocacy

The Indian judiciary relies heavily on an oral advocacy culture—an oral hearing in person is considered the norm and any deviations remain the exception. Perhaps the only place where this equation is reversed is with review petitions—petitions filed before the Court to review its own decisions—which are considered extraordinarily exceptional, to be permitted only when there is an error apparent on the face of the record or when new evidence has come to light, or for similar exceptional reasons.[61] The Supreme Court has put in place these high thresholds for invoking the review jurisdiction through its own rules and judgments.[62] While recently the Court appears to have diluted the standard for entertaining reviews from writ petitions,[63] overall, the review petitioner has a high bar to meet to convince the Court to re-examine its judgment.

The process for deciding a review petition also mirrors the exceptional nature of this power. Petitioners file the petition clearly stating the grounds for review. Review petitions are decided by circulating the documents of the case without an oral hearing. Only in exceptional cases, where judges are inclined to admit the matter or where the review pertains to the imposition of the death penalty, does the Court allow for an in-person hearing in open court.

Thus, the preliminary screening is based on documentary evidence, and only upon the high bar being met, does the matter move to open court. In reviews against judgments imposing the death penalty, the process has been changed to reflect the need for a lower threshold for reviewing such decisions, given the extraordinary nature of the punishment. All reviews from such cases are mandatorily heard in open court. The difference in these two approaches indicates that the process can be tailored to reflect different thresholds for entertaining petitions of different kinds.

The review jurisdiction is considered extraordinary, stringently controlled, and rarely granted, for many of the same reasons that we are advocating for a restricted SLP jurisdiction—to keep the docket in check, to ensure finality and certainty of decisions, and to ensure that cases do not drag on unnecessarily, while also allowing for some leeway to correct grave errors and account for human fallibility.

Applying a similar framework to the admission docket for appeals, one could construct a system for SLPs to be decided by circulation. If even one judge on a bench is inclined to admit the matter, notice may be issued to the other side and the matter would be posted for an oral hearing. Such a method will have the additional advantage of reducing the influence of the 'face value' of senior advocates in the admissions process and thus give all cases a fair shot at being decided on merits. (We discuss the 'face value' of senior advocates in Chapter 3.)

An objection could be raised that a documentary-only admissions process may not provide enough guidance to judges to make fair decisions or that it may lead to opacity in the process, with litigants not knowing why their case was denied leave. But even today, cases that are dismissed at the threshold of the admissions stage are decided without giving reasons. And, each admissions matter gets on average ninety-three seconds of the Court's time—hardly enough to make an in-depth argument. Where the Court is inclined to admit, or thinks there is merit in a second look—it can post the matter for an oral hearing, as it does in review cases. To make the case for this approach, the Court could try it out on specific classes of cases—where all the lower courts have agreed as to the decision under challenge for instance, or for certain subject matters.

Another way to reduce backlogs is to institute time limits for oral arguments during merit hearings. Although lawyers get hardly any time to argue at the admission stage, once the matter is admitted, there are generally no time limits for how long the lawyer may be permitted to argue. Unlike many courts in other parts of the world, how long a lawyer gets to argue their case before the Indian Supreme Court depends entirely on the bench. The 'face value' of the lawyer influences, though does not entirely determine, the time allocated to each party. One fallout of this approach is that litigants and lawyers have little certainty when, or if at all, their matters will 'reach' the bench on a day when the matter is listed. Set time limits, either applicable across the board or determined in advance for each individual case, can redress these concerns, while also ensuring that cases progress in a timely manner. This would again require a move away from the 'oral advocacy' culture of Indian courts to a greater reliance on documentary practices. The time in court would then be limited to making the main points in a case, highlighting areas that a judge ought to pay special attention to and clarifying questions from the bench. In exceptional cases, the Court may of course extend the time permitted to each party to argue their matter. Time limits will have the additional benefit of giving relatively junior or unknown lawyers as much of a chance to shine in court as senior lawyers and break the hierarchy prevalent in the bar.

Again, the implementation of these recommendations is likely to face stiff opposition from the bar because the bar benefits from the status quo—even if their clients do not. In the spirit of demonstrating the benefits of such a model, the Court may consider a 'model court' approach where a specific bench of the Supreme Court is allowed to institute these rules, to examine the efficacy of the system.

A Litigation Policy for Government Litigation

A final policy shift that can make an impact on backlogs is for the government to change its approach to litigation. Today the government is by far the biggest litigant before the Supreme Court. It is an appellant in almost 73 per cent of all admitted matters.[64] However, our data shows that the government has an indifferent success rate across many subject matter categories, which indicates that it needs better mechanisms to decide which cases to appeal.[65] Nearly one in every five matters admitted by the Supreme Court where the government is an appellant, pertains to a tax matter. However, the government has less than a 50 per cent chance of winning in such cases—worse odds than flipping a coin. And these odds are in admitted matters, which excludes the many others that do not even make it to this stage. This implies that the government could do with better filtering of such cases internally. Criminal matters too constitute a large bulk of admitted matters where the government is an appellant—these are cases where the government is either appealing against an acquittal or appealing for the enhancement of a sentence. Once admitted, the government has slightly better than fifty-fifty odds of securing reversal of the lower-court judgment in criminal matters. Again, this data only accounts for admitted cases. We do not have data for cases that are denied admission, but accounting for them would bring the government's success rate down significantly. What we can say with certainty is that the government has a liberal appeals filing policy in criminal cases and needs better filtering mechanisms. (Table 4 lists the government's rate of success (the reversal rate) for different types of cases when it is the appellant in the Supreme Court.)

Rank	Subject Matter Category	Share (in per cent)	Reversal Rate (in per cent)
1	Service Matters	19.2	67.3
2	Criminal Matters	17.3	56.8
3	Indirect Taxes Matters	10.8	50.3
4	Ordinary Civil Matters	8.9	66.4
5	Direct Taxes Matters	6.9	48.4
6	Land Acquisition & Requisition Matters	6.4	74.1
7	Constitutional Matters[66]	5.5	100
8	Academic Matters	2.3	13.8
9	Arbitration Matters	2.1	65.5
10	Appeal Against Orders of Statutory Body	2.1	72.4

Table 4: Reversal rates where government is the appellant, by subject matter

At the national level, a long-proposed National Litigation Policy was introduced in 2010 but remained unenforced. In 2015, a new National Litigation Policy was attempted but this too has not seen the light of day. Framing such a policy with rigorous in-house mechanisms for determining which cases to appeal may go a long way towards bringing down the volume of cases on the Supreme Court's docket. A major reason for indiscriminate appeals by the government is that the officer who decides whether or not to appeal does not have to bear the costs of filing a weak appeal, but may bear consequences if no appeal is filed in a case deemed 'appeal-worthy' by senior officers. At best, the officer might expect formal or informal censure for dereliction of duty. At worst, allegations of corruption may be levelled against the officer. To avoid these consequences, officers often prefer to file an appeal even when the government's case is weak. Changing this incentive structure by removing decision-making on appeals from the officer most directly connected with that matter and seeking an independent review of the case to determine likelihood of success may reduce government litigation.

A National Court of Appeals?

Finally, a solution that *is* being considered by the Court on the judicial side and which has its own advocates[67] is neither necessary nor advisable. In a matter pending before a Constitution Bench, the Supreme Court is considering the advisability of setting up a National Court of Appeals to decide appeals cases that currently reach the Supreme Court.[68] (Ironically, a three-judge bench of the Supreme Court referred the matter to a Constitution Bench in 2016. As of this writing, this case has not been assigned to any Constitution Bench, much less come up for hearing even once in the intervening years).

Proponents of this policy argue that a National Court of Appeals could free up the Supreme Court to focus on constitutional matters and other matters of great public and legal significance. In theory, this sounds good. In practice, such an approach just shifts the site of the problem, without addressing the problem itself. A National Court of Appeals is likely to be as overrun by cases as the Supreme Court, if it retains the same standards for admitting appeals. Even worse, if the Supreme Court then retains the Article 136 power and allows appeals from such a National Court of Appeals, it will just add another intermediate layer to the judicial system, without solving the issue of backlogs and worsening delays. And if the National Court of Appeals has a more restrictive admissions criteria, then there is no reason why the Supreme Court itself cannot adopt such standards. In sum, there is little evidence to support the need for a National Court of Appeals.

Conclusion

It is well-known that cases take a long time to resolve in the Indian court system. What is less known is that the source of the delay is not just the lower courts. Delays are also endemic at the Supreme Court. Our analysis of five years of Supreme Court decisions further finds that there is a two-track system with certain cases being resolved much faster than other cases. There is no doubt that part of the reason that it takes a long time to get a case resolved in the Supreme Court is because over the years the number of cases filed has increased exponentially. But that is not the only explanation. The Court has also admitted more cases over time for full consideration through a mechanism known as the 'special leave petition'.

To speed up justice, the Parliament has resorted to increasing the judge capacity of the Court. Yet, that has not solved the problem. Instead of increasing the supply of judges, we suggest that the Court decrease the supply of cases it takes by being more selective in its SLP admissions. This will both reduce the Court's caseload, giving the judges more capacity to issue reasoned decisions in a timely manner. Better reasoned cases will also give better guidance to lower courts to resolve cases. We also propose making more decisions, particularly admissions decisions, without oral hearings and when the Court does hear cases orally, setting time limits on the hearings. Finally, the government, which has the greatest number of cases before the Court as compared to any other litigant, can alleviate the problem being more selective about which cases it appeals.

3

'Face Value': The Power and Influence of Senior Advocates

A senior advocate filed a special leave petition with the Supreme Court, and at the admission hearing, a judge asked, 'Is there any merit in your case?' He answered, 'Your lordship, I flew all the way from the UK to appear at this hearing. I would not have done that if there were no merit.' The SLP was admitted.[1]

'Senior Advocate' is a title of great distinction for a lawyer in India. Individually appointed by the Supreme Court or by state high courts, senior advocates enjoy prestige and command princely fees. Some can charge Rs 15 lakh for an admissions hearing (like the hearing described above) that lasts on average, less than two minutes. The story above may be an extreme example, but talk to any judge or lawyer who knows the Supreme Court well and sooner or later, you will hear their own first-hand account of the unusual influence that senior advocates have in the Supreme Court.

Indeed, the sway that senior advocates have with the Supreme Court is not only the subject of countless anecdotes but of empirical research studies too. As we will explain in this chapter, the hard data tells the same story as the anecdotes. For parties that can afford the fees, a senior advocate provides an easier path to admission to the Supreme Court.

Is this a problem? The story of the senior advocate who flew in from the United Kingdom shows how the power of senior advocates could be a good or bad thing. A positive interpretation of the story is that highly skilled lawyers are good judges of what makes a case important and meritorious. A senior advocate is more likely to accept as a client, someone with an important and meritorious case. And as a highly skilled lawyer, the senior advocate can then persuasively explain the case's merit to the Court. Thus, when a senior advocate appears on behalf of a petition, this helps to inform the Court that the petition is likely meritorious, and the Court is more willing to admit the case for a full hearing on the merits. In this interpretation, it is a good thing that the Court prefers to admit cases represented by top lawyers, as it helps the Court devote attention to the strongest petitions and best legal arguments.

The negative interpretation of the story is obvious. The judges unquestioningly accept the word of the senior advocate—either because they know her personally or because the judges are dazzled by the lawyer's reputation. If this is the case, the senior advocate isn't helping the Court pick better cases or write better judgments but is greasing the wheels of justice for those who are rich enough to pay her fees. In this process, the Court gains nothing. In fact, the senior advocate might be fooling the Court into taking a weak petition with poor legal arguments.

Which interpretation is closer to the truth? Of course, if you ask judges and senior advocates, they are likely to tell you the positive story.[2] If you ask critics of the Court, they are likely to tell you the negative story. Anecdotes alone can't tell us what is behind the Court's possible favouritism toward senior advocates.

In this chapter, we use data to answer this question. Using the research of others and our own data, we explore how much power senior advocates have and where it comes from. Our data indicates that, despite being among the top legal minds in India, senior advocates aren't making the Supreme Court's decisions better. More often than not, they're making them worse.

We then offer what might be a surprising proposal for remedying this perverse state of affairs. Our solution is *not* to reduce the influence of senior advocates. As a practical matter, it would be impossible to eliminate the influence of the most accomplished and well-connected lawyers and it wouldn't be a good idea to do this either. Senior advocates are highly skilled lawyers, and highly skilled lawyers *should* get more attention from the Court. Instead, as we will explain in this chapter, the Court's process for admitting and hearing cases should be changed, so that senior advocates have the right incentives to use their skills to help the Court make better judgments, rather than admit worse cases.

Handpicked Stars of the Bar

'Senior advocate' is a designation conferred by the Supreme Court or one of the high courts and is thus, highly prestigious. A designation as a senior advocate welcomes one into an exclusive elite group in the Indian legal profession, representing less than 1 per cent of lawyers in India.

Senior advocates occupy a special role in litigation. They do not work directly with clients. Instead, they interact with the briefing counsel. The briefing counsel directly represents the client and makes arrangements on behalf of the client for the senior advocate to argue in court. Senior advocates do not file cases in the Supreme Court—that is the role of the Advocate-on-Record or AOR. Under the rules of the Supreme Court, only an AOR may file a matter in the Supreme Court. Like 'senior advocate', 'advocate-on-record' is a special designation conferred by the Supreme Court. To become an AOR, an attorney must pass a qualification examination administered by the Supreme Court. Unlike senior advocates, however, AORs do not necessarily make courtroom appearances or argue cases. Instead, the AOR files the court papers and advises the senior advocate on the matter.

Senior advocates therefore have a highly specialized role. They are the courtroom advocates who appear for court hearings and make oral arguments. Interacting with clients, filing petitions and other court documents, and scheduling hearings are handled by other advocates.[3] This specialized role allows the senior advocate to devote a large amount of working time to courtroom appearances. This in turn means that senior advocates accumulate a huge amount of experience at the Supreme Court and are constantly in front of the judges. They are familiar faces that the judges of the Court see regularly in the courtroom.

Senior advocates are famed for their legal knowledge and oratory skills. They are also famous for their staggering fees. It is typical for senior advocates to charge between Rs 1 and 5 lakh for a single appearance in the Supreme Court. An advocate can appear at multiple hearings in a single day, especially on Mondays and Fridays, when the Court holds hearings to admit or dismiss special leave petitions (SLPs). Indeed, for many senior advocates, the bulk of their business comes from appearances at admissions hearings.[4]

At an admissions hearing, the Court decides whether to admit an SLP (putting it on the path to a full hearing on the merits of the case) or to dismiss it. These hearings are very brief. For senior advocates in high demand, it is not unusual to appear at as many as twelve admissions hearings in one day. In 2015, one of the top senior advocates, Gopal Jain, indicated that he typically would charge Rs 2 or 3 lakh for an admissions hearing and would typically do six or seven hearings in a day.[5]

Jain is an example of the most elite among the senior advocates, whom scholars Marc Galanter and Nick Robinson have called 'India's Grand Advocates'. For their lofty standing, influence and exclusive ranks, the grand advocates have no equal in the world. They comprise the forty or fifty senior advocates who are 'giants and legends of the litigation system'.[6] They command fees commensurate with their ultra-elite status and media coverage compares them to Bollywood celebrities.[7] Ram Jethmalani, who retired in 2017 and passed away in 2019, was widely regarded as the greatest senior advocate of his day and could command more than Rs 25 lakh per hearing. Other grand advocates charge Rs 15 lakh or higher for a single hearing.[8]

These top senior advocates tend be older, with decades of experience in law practice, politics and government. They also tend to be highly connected politically. Examples from recent years of grand

advocates with extensive experience in politics include the late Ram
Jethmalani (former Minister of Law and Justice), P. Chidambaram
(former Minister of Finance and current member of Parliament),
Fali S. Nariman (former Rajya Sabha member), Kapil Sibal (former
Minister of Law and Justice and current member of Parliament),
Abhishek Manu Singhvi (Member of Parliament) and Harish Salve
(former Solicitor General).

The elite status of senior advocates and the super-elite, celebrity
status of grand advocates reflects the stratification of the legal profession
more generally. Galanter and Robinson describe 'a long-standing
and pervasive pattern of steep hierarchy at the bar. At every level, the
provision of legal services was (and is) dominated by a small number of
lawyers with outsized reputations, who have the lion's share of clients,
income, prestige, standing and influence'.[9]

Despite their prominence and prestige, senior advocates have been
criticized for contributing to the chronic delays in the Supreme Court—a
claim for which we will provide additional data in this chapter. In their
research on senior advocates, Galanter and Robinson confirmed the
conclusions reached years before by famed sociologist T.K. Oommen,
who observed that the pre-eminence of senior advocates and the culture
of delays in the judiciary went hand in hand. The top senior advocates
have so much business that they often commit to more hearings than
they can attend. To manage this workload, the grand advocates seek
and are granted court adjournments.[10]

Why do judges allow this? It is because, as Oommen concluded
(and Galanter and Robinson agreed), 'the leading lawyers rather
than the judges, emerge as norm-setters and value-givers in the court
system.'[11] And why do the lawyers, not the judges, set the norms?
The prestige and power of the senior advocates come from their
long-standing relationships with the Court and the judges. As judges
informed George Gadbois, the Supreme Court 'bar was powerful and
vocal' which made some judges 'afraid of the bar', and 'they tried to
please senior advocates'.[12]

Further, senior advocates have seniority and experience that may
exceed even the judges themselves. The judge may feel deference to the

greater seniority of the senior advocate, who may have *decades* more experience in the Supreme Court than the judge. As Galanter and Robinson put it: 'Often Supreme Court judges are not only younger than the senior advocates who argue before them, but the judges may have looked up to these advocates when they themselves were young lawyers.'[13]

This is an important but unintended consequence of how judges are appointed and when they retire. Judicial appointment to the Supreme Court depends in large part on seniority within the judiciary. As discussed in Chapter 4, judges appointed to the Supreme Court are almost invariably in their late fifties or early sixties.[14] Before appointment, most Supreme Court judges have spent their careers as judges in various courts throughout India—not practising as lawyers in the Supreme Court. Further, judges are subject to mandatory retirement at age sixty-five in the Supreme Court. Thus, the typical Supreme Court judge, by the time he or she retires, will have about five or six years' experience in the Supreme Court.[15]

In contrast, a senior advocate could end his or her career with five or six *decades'* experience in the Supreme Court. There are no age limits on the practice of law. A senior advocate may begin his career as an advocate in the Supreme Court in his twenties or thirties and continue practising until the end of his life. Thus, it is understandable that even a Supreme Court judge would feel a degree of awe toward a lawyer who knows the Supreme Court far better than the justice ever will. The most striking example of this is Ram Jethmalani, who was amongst the highest-paid and oldest senior advocates when he retired in 2017 at age ninety-three. Jethmalani had risen to national prominence in 1959 prosecuting K.M. Nanavati, a naval officer accused of murdering his wife's lover.[16] In other words, Jethmalani had been a nationally-famous lawyer since before many current judges of the Supreme Court were even born!

Gatekeepers to the Court

Although it is widely believed that senior advocates wield influence over the Supreme Court's decisions at all stages of a case, it is at the very start of a case in the Supreme Court that their power appears greatest. As we've noted, the vast majority (more than 80 per cent) of the cases seeking review in the Supreme Court come to the Court as SLPs, which the Court can freely choose to admit or dismiss.[17]

It is at this initial hearing stage that most petitions are turned away without another hearing. And it is at this stage, where the Court exercises wide discretion on which cases to admit, that senior advocates are most active. One study found that although senior advocates are less than 1 per cent of the bar, they appeared in nearly 40 per cent of initial hearings for SLPs.[18]

The frequent presence of senior advocates at SLP admission hearings puts the senior advocates in the role of gatekeepers to the Supreme Court—they are the ones influencing the Court on which cases to admit. Of course, senior advocates are only effective as gatekeepers if the Court heeds their advice. But by all accounts, the Court does.

A widely circulated study by the Vidhi Centre for Legal Policy shows exactly how much success senior advocates have as the gatekeepers to the Court. Researchers at the Vidhi Centre collected a sample of 290 cases from 2014 in which the Supreme Court held an initial hearing on a special leave petition. For the petitioner, success meant the Court 'issuing notice'—entering an order that allowed the case to continue to the next stage. Failure was dismissal of the petition—the case in the Supreme Court was over.

The Vidhi Centre researchers compared the success rate for petitions in which a senior advocate appeared on behalf of the petitioner to the success rate of petitions without a senior advocate. Although the study relied on a limited sample of cases, its results were nonetheless striking.[19] When a senior advocate appeared in court to argue for the petitioner, the success rate nearly doubled:

- Success rate for SLPs *with* senior advocates: 60 per cent
- Success rate for SLPs *without* senior advocates: 34 per cent

In other words, it appears that senior advocates have a distinct advantage in getting petitions admitted. And with the fate of a case riding on the outcome of a single hearing, it should be no surprise that senior advocates earn huge fees for their appearances. As the Vidhi Centre researchers noted, in 2015, senior advocates earned between Rs 75,000 and 16.5 lakh per hearing in the Supreme Court—and remember, these are on average less than two-minute hearings![20]

We now turn to the question of *why* senior advocates have so much more success than other advocates. Is it because they bring better cases—cases that deserve to be heard by the Supreme Court—or is it that they influence the Court (either because of their persuasive skill or their reputation) to take cases that it really shouldn't be hearing?

Why Do Senior Advocates Have Power over the Court's Docket?

As we noted at the outset of this chapter, the fact that senior advocates hold great sway over the Court may or may not be a good thing. On the one hand, senior advocates could be skilled at bringing the most meritorious petitions to the Court. They could raise the strongest and most thoroughly reasoned legal arguments. On the other hand, it could be that the judges of the Court favour senior advocates, due to familiarity, admiration or other factors unrelated to the merits of the case or the quality of the arguments that they bring.

Prior empirical work, such as the Vidhi Centre study, has shown the wide gap between the success rates of senior advocates and other lawyers, but has *not* been able to show why senior advocates have so much more success.[21] By combining past research with our new data, we can now show why. In the sections that follow, we present two explanations for senior advocates' success that are *not* supported by the data and one explanation that fits the data better. With the benefit of our data, the overall picture becomes clearer—senior advocates aren't helping the Court choose the best cases or find the clearest legal rules. If anything, it is the opposite.

Two Stories that Don't Work

We begin with the two reasons it would be a good thing for the Supreme Court to favour petitions brought by senior advocates. In short, they are that (1) senior advocates make better legal arguments, and (2) senior advocates bring better cases. We find that while it is surely true that the senior advocates are skilled at legal argumentation and at judging the merit of a petition, these factors *aren't* primarily what is driving their success in the Supreme Court.

Do the Senior Advocates Make Better Legal Arguments?

The first possibility is easy to dispose of. While most senior advocates surely are experts at legal reasoning, their ability to help the Court identify or create legal rules is only useful if the Court is trying to identify or create legal rules. But most of the Court's judgments are not focused on affirming existing legal rules or announcing new ones. As we've noted, most Supreme Court opinions contain *no* citations to legal precedent and do not announce legal rules that are ever cited again by a future Supreme Court opinion.[22] (Of course, senior advocates may make legal arguments to the Court that help the Court reach its decisions, but if so, most of the Court's judgments make no mention of this.)

The Supreme Court *could* focus its energies on admitting SLPs with the goal of writing a judicial opinion that identifies legal precedent and announces clear legal rules. And if it did, the greater skill of senior advocates would be a sensible reason for the Court to give favourable treatment to petitions brought by senior advocates (we'll return to this possibility later). For now, even though senior advocates surely are skilled at legal reasoning, this does not explain why the Supreme Court grants their petitions.

Do the Best Advocates Bring the Best Cases?

The second story might seem more plausible. As we argued in Chapter 1, the Supreme Court considers itself a 'people's court', committed to granting access to deserving petitioners and ensuring that justice is done. As a consequence, it would make sense for the judges of the Court to look for any signal that a petition has merit, even if that signal is simply the fact that a senior advocate thought it worthwhile to take the case. To paraphrase the quote at the beginning of this chapter, a senior advocate won't fly from the UK to appear at a hearing unless the petition has merit. So, the argument goes, the Court should take the senior advocate's word for it.

Thanks to our data, however, we don't have to take anyone's word for it. We use our data on SLP hearings and final case outcomes to see whether senior advocates were bringing cases with better merit than other advocates. How do we do this? The logic goes like this:

We start with the hypothesis that senior advocates bring stronger petitions than other advocates. In other words, the cases brought by senior advocates are cases that are more likely to win if the Supreme Court admits them for a full hearing. The Supreme Court, of course, does not want to waste its time admitting petitions that are going to lose on the merits anyway. It is better to dismiss them at the initial hearing. Thus, if senior advocates tend to get the strongest cases, then the Supreme Court prefers to admit petitions brought by senior advocates.

If all of this is true, then the data on SLP cases should show that SLPs brought by senior advocates are *both* more successful at the initial admissions stage *and* more successful at eventually winning a full hearing in the Supreme Court. In other words, if senior advocates bring higher quality petitions than other advocates, those petitions shouldn't just do better at the initial, two-minute hearing, they should do well once the court takes the time to study the case.

Is this true? To study this question, we collected two kinds of data on Supreme Court cases. First, we examined the full case records from a sample of 466 SLPs filed with the Supreme Court in 2010.[23] We chose 2010, because we wanted a year far enough in the past that we could see what eventually happened to the petitions after filing in the Supreme Court—which usually takes years. Our research has found that the *average* time it takes for a case to reach a final judgment after a full hearing in the Supreme Court is longer than four years, with many cases taking twice as long or longer.[24]

For this sample, we first looked to see whether senior advocates have more success than other advocates at convincing the Supreme

Court to admit SLPs for further hearings.[25] Similar to the Vidhi Centre study, we find that senior advocates did have higher success rates at initial hearings:

- Initial hearing success rate for senior advocates: 35 per cent
- Initial hearing success rate for other advocates: 28 per cent

Further, our data confirms that the initial hearing is the key moment in the case for a petition seeking a full hearing from the Supreme Court. Technically, success at the initial hearing usually only guarantees another hearing on whether to admit the petition ('issuing notice', as we described above). It doesn't guarantee that the petition will survive all the way to a full hearing at which the Court can grant the petitioner a victory in the case. But as a *practical* matter, success at the initial hearing almost guarantees a more extensive hearing. In our data, of all the petitions that succeeded in the initial hearing, 88 per cent of them eventually reached a full hearing for the petitioner's claims.[26] In other words, although petitions usually must survive multiple hearings before the petitioner has a chance to win on their claim, in most cases, it is only the first hearing that matters. Lose there, and the case is over. Win there, and the path to a full hearing is almost assured.

We then looked at whether the cases that survived the initial hearing turned out to be winners after the Court eventually held a full, final hearing. This is not something that other researchers have yet explored. In this sample, SLPs that had been brought by senior advocates were more likely to win than SLPs brought by other advocates:

- Final hearing win rate for SLPs brought by senior advocates: 40 per cent
- Final hearing win rate for SLPs brought by other advocates: 29 per cent

This evidence is a point in favour of the interpretation that senior advocates bring higher quality cases. Senior advocates do have higher success rates at getting the Supreme Court to admit a petition, but this makes sense if the cases brought by senior advocates are cases that the Supreme Court, in the end, decides are winners. But there are two problems with this conclusion. First, the data is also consistent with the possibility that they don't bring better cases—they are just better at persuading the Court to decide in their favour. Our data cannot rule out that possibility.

More importantly, though, this pattern doesn't hold up in other data. In addition to our sample SLPs filed in 2010 that we followed through to the final judgment, we also collected all final judgments published by the Supreme Court from 2010–2014. A team of research assistants read all these judgments and recorded whether the petitioner won and whether the petitioner was represented by a senior advocate.[27] In the end, we had a sample of more than 5000 cases from the Supreme Court for which we had information on whether the petitioner was represented by a senior advocate.

This dataset does not contain information on initial hearings. It only contains information on final hearings—who were the lawyers and which side won. Thus, this data cannot tell us whether senior advocates are better at getting cases admitted to the Supreme Court. But this data can tell us whether cases with senior advocates are more likely to be winners in the Supreme Court.

Contrary to the pattern in our smaller sample from 2010, we find that the answer is no.[28] In fact, senior advocates had a *lower* win rate than other advocates:

- Win rate for petitioners with senior advocates: 57 per cent
- Win rate for petitioners with other advocates: 60 per cent

This casts doubts on the idea that the Supreme Court favours SLPs brought by senior advocates because senior advocates identify stronger cases and bring them to the attention of the Court. If anything, our five years of data suggest the opposite—senior advocates, on average, represent weaker cases.[29]

To be clear: our data does not prove that senior advocates bring *worse* cases than other advocates. Rather, our data calls into question the idea that the Supreme Court favours senior advocates because they bring *better* cases. The evidence just isn't there.

* * *

So far, we have examined two possible reasons for why the Supreme Court seems to favour cases brought by senior advocates for admission to the Court. The first is that senior advocates help the Court find precedent and identify good legal rules. The second is that senior advocates bring stronger cases, and that is why senior advocates have more of their cases admitted. Both stories describe a valuable function that senior advocates *could* serve—but they don't fit the data on how the Court *actually* operates. Now we turn to a final explanation for why senior advocates have an edge in the Supreme Court. This explanation fits the data that we've presented in this chapter.

One Story that Works

We now turn to a very different story for why senior advocates have a clear advantage in getting their cases admitted to the Supreme Court. It goes like this—the Supreme Court hears tens of thousands of petitions per year. Even with more than thirty hard-working judges, this is a staggering amount of work. Unable to devote careful attention to each of these cases, the judges of the Supreme Court are desperate to find ways to admit or dismiss petitions as fast as possible. One way to manage the time crunch is to rely on what they do know—the lawyers in front of them. And no lawyers are more familiar to the Court, and more trusted by the Court, than senior advocates. Sometimes, in the span of a two-minute hearing, the judges can tell whether a petition has true merit or not, and they admit or dismiss accordingly. But often, they cannot tell. In those cases, they decide based on the advocate. It is easy to say, 'dismissed', to a stranger, but it is hard to turn away a familiar face, a celebrity or a respected elder.

An Overwhelmed Court Looking for Familiar Faces

We begin with the fact that the judges of the Supreme Court face a crushing case load. As we described in Chapter 1, the Court's pursuit of being a 'people's court' has led it to invite a massive flow of SLPs that it must sift through. The Court receives over 60,000 petitions per year. It devotes two days per week—Monday and Friday—to hearings on whether to admit or dismiss these petitions. And because it holds at least one hearing per petition, and sometimes more, before admitting or dismissing the petition, this means that on any given Monday or Friday, the Court holds around 1000 hearings.

The judges of the Supreme Court must somehow sort through this mountain of cases. To do this, it divides itself into benches of two judges to hear each petition, allowing it to hold many hearings in tandem throughout the day. And it holds incredibly compressed hearings. As we've noted, most hearings on SLPs last one minute and thirty-three seconds or *less*.[30] In other words, in a typical case, the judges hear the law, facts and arguments relevant to the case for less than 100 seconds before they make their decision.

Yet, as our data shows, the initial hearing for an SLP is the most crucial hearing for a case seeking relief in the Supreme Court. A petition that makes it past this first step is nearly guaranteed a full hearing by the Court and a chance at winning the case in a final judgment. How can judges make such a momentous decision after a hearing that lasts less than two minutes?

The answer, of course, is that two minutes is simply not enough time to have an adequate hearing of the relevant facts, legal issues, case history and arguments by the petitioner. Yet every Monday and Friday, the Supreme Court makes admissions decisions on hundreds of cases on the basis of less than two minutes of hearing time. With so little time per case, the Supreme Court must make snap decisions, and one piece of information that it always has when making that decision is the identity of the lawyer making the argument.

Given these facts, it should be no surprise that senior advocates are so valuable to the Supreme Court. They represent familiarity, trust, experience and knowledge in a setting where hard facts, legal details and time are in short supply. A senior advocate arguing before two Supreme Court judges at an admissions hearing is likely going to have more experience in the Supreme Court than both of the judges combined. From day one on the Supreme Court until retirement day, a Supreme Court judge will see the same senior advocates again and again. Even if the bias is unconscious, it would only be natural for a judge to defer to a familiar face who has much more experience than the judge has.

This deference is natural, but it is also a problem. The senior advocate has credibility due to experience and expertise but isn't likely giving an objective assessment of the worthiness of the petition. The senior advocate is an *advocate*, who is highly paid to obtain a specific result from the Court. Further, the initial admissions hearing is not a balanced hearing, where both sides are heard. Usually, only the counsel for the petitioner is present.

Further, the power of the senior advocate is not available to all. With rates exceeding Rs 15 lakh for the most prominent senior advocates, this power is available only to the very rich. To be sure, many senior advocates offer their services at reduced rates or even free as a *pro bono* service to clients who are less wealthy, but this charity is exercised at the discretion of the senior advocate. In other words, the decision of who gains access to the Supreme Court is once again in the hands of the senior advocate.

How Did the Supreme Court Get Here?

This is not a good state of affairs. As we have shown, there is little evidence that the power of senior advocates is about the valuable skills they *could* provide—giving the Court better legal rules and better cases. Instead, it seems that the Court's preferential treatment of senior advocates is more about a bias towards familiar, respected individuals, regardless of the merits of the petitions. How did we get to this point? One explanation is the Court's enormous docket of SLPs. The Court is desperate to sort through them, so the judges simply defer to senior advocates. Thus, we see the 'face value' of senior advocates—simply by showing up to the Supreme Court, they give their clients an advantage in getting admission to further hearings.

Importantly, the crushing load of petitions is partly due to the Court's own policies and how lawyers have reacted to them. In this section, we show how three key groups have contributed to the extreme number of petitions:

- *The Supreme Court*: Its failure to set clear guidelines for when an SLP will be admitted invites more SLPs.
- *Advocates on Record*: Because AORs are paid by the case, they have incentives to file as many petitions as possible.
- *Senior Advocates*: Their ability to get SLPs admitted, even when the case is weak, means that parties with weak cases find it worthwhile to file SLPs.

The Supreme Court: Turning the SLP into a Lottery Ticket

As we've noted, the Supreme Court has not set clear guidelines for when it will admit or deny a special leave petition. Further, it admits a large fraction of SLPs, almost 15 per cent. Together, these facts mean that every litigant has a chance at getting a petition admitted at the Supreme Court. Big cases, small cases, easy cases, hard cases, clear law, unclear law, important questions, unimportant questions—everything is fair game for admission to the Supreme Court!

Thus, any party who has lost their case in the high court but can afford paying more legal fees, may find it worthwhile to file an SLP. With millions of cases pending in the high courts, it is no surprise that the Supreme Court receives tens of thousands of petitions every year. This, in turn, means that the Supreme Court faces so many petitions that it simply cannot spend more than a few minutes on each one.

The AOR System: It Pays to File More Petitions

As we described at the beginning of this chapter, the Supreme Court separates the filing of petitions from the arguing of cases. Advocates on Record file petitions and set cases for argument, but they do not usually argue the cases. The lucrative fees for appearances go to senior advocates. AORs cannot charge as much per case, because they do not offer influential face time with the judges. The income of an AOR depends primarily on filing more cases, not on charging a lot per case. A successful practice for an AOR, therefore, requires filing lots of cases. For AORs, the more petitions filed, the better!

Senior Advocate Influence: Both Cause and Effect of the Heavy Caseload

So far in this chapter, we have argued that the heavy caseload of the Court is an explanation for why senior advocates have so much influence on the Court. It is also the case that the influence of senior advocates contributes to the heavy caseload. As senior advocates have the ability to influence the Supreme Court's decisions to admit SLPs, parties with weak cases can get a decent chance at admission if they retain a senior advocate. This is yet another reason why the Supreme Court faces so many SLPs. Parties with weak or borderline cases will file a petition anyway, knowing that hiring a senior advocate gives them a realistic chance at admission.

In this way, senior advocates contribute to a self-reinforcing cycle: The Supreme Court faces too many SLPs. It relies on senior advocates to decide which ones to admit. Because senior advocates hold sway with the Court, litigants with weak petitions retain senior advocates to argue their SLPs, further increasing the number of SLPs. As the numbers of SLPs rise, the Court must rely on senior advocates even more. And so on and so on.

Putting Senior Advocate Power to Good Use

It is no surprise that we find that senior advocates—the hand-picked stars of the Supreme Court bar—exercise influence over which cases the Supreme Court chooses to hear. More surprising is our answer to *why* senior advocates get special attention from the Court. Even though senior advocates presumably have great skill at legal research and assessing the merits of cases, we don't find evidence that the Court relies on senior advocates to find better legal rules or separate weak cases from strong cases. Instead, our research suggests that the Court gravitates toward cases brought by senior advocates as a way to sort through the overwhelming number of SLPs being filed with the Court.

Why is the Court overwhelmed with cases? As we explained, the Court's lax standards for admitting petitions, AORs' incentives to file large numbers of cases with the Court and senior advocates' ability to make even weak petitions viable, all combine to encourage anyone who can afford it to file an SLP.

But there is a paradox here. As we showed in Chapter 1, the Court has lax standards for granting SLPs because it wants to be a 'people's court', a court that allows access to petitioners, no matter how humble. Yet as we have just showed, senior advocates are the key players who get SLPs admitted to the Supreme Court. And senior advocates are the most expensive lawyers in India—and some of them are the most expensive lawyers in the world! Only the rich and powerful can afford to pay Rs 15 lakh for a lawyer to appear at a two-minute hearing.

In other words, the Supreme Court's approach to SLPs seeks to favour the common person for access to the Court, but at the same time, the Court heavily favours SLPs argued by the most expensive lawyers in the country. The Court gives access with one hand and takes it away with the other. It is working at cross purposes with itself.

This is neither good for the Court nor good for parties seeking access to the Court. By welcoming an onslaught of SLPs, the Court ensures that it does not have time left to spend on careful deliberation on petitions or on writing judicial opinions that announce clear rules for other courts to follow. The quality of the Court's decision-making and its ability to lead the Indian courts suffers.

This might be an acceptable price to pay if its willingness to admit thousands of petitions meant that the cost of access to the Court was low, and common people had easy access to justice. But as we've seen, the opposite is true—the gatekeepers of the Court are high-priced senior advocates.

Therefore, as we conclude our Chapter on senior advocates, we offer a vision for fixing the relationship between senior advocates and the Supreme Court. Our argument proceeds in three simple steps:

- *Don't resist the power of senior advocates*: A practical solution cannot seek to reduce the influence of senior advocates. Their influence is deeply embedded in the Court and there are good reasons why they should continue to have influence.
- *Focus on their legal expertise*: The Supreme Court should pursue reforms that channel the power of senior advocates in new directions. The legal expertise of senior advocates is an underutilized resource for improving the Supreme Court's effectiveness in deciding cases and announcing legal rules.
- *Create rules that reward expertise, not prestige*: Strict and clear guidelines for when the Court will admit an SLP will reduce the flood of petitions, allow judges to spend more time on each case, and permit advocates (including senior advocates) to focus on developing high-quality legal arguments that the Court can use in deciding cases. Raising the retirement age of Supreme Court judges will reduce the seniority imbalance between senior advocates and judges as further discussed in Chapter 5.

In short, the solution is not to reduce the power of senior advocates—this is probably impossible anyway—but to change *how* and *why* they have power. As we described at the outset, a possible explanation for the influence of senior advocates is that they help the Court identify important cases and announce clear legal rulings. This isn't primarily what senior advocates are doing *now*, but they could be and should be. Senior advocates are the most powerful actors in the current system and they can be the most powerful force for positive change.

Don't Resist the Power of Senior Advocates

We've emphasized the influence that senior advocates have in the Supreme Court. We've described how this influence contributes to the congestion of the Court's docket. And we've shown that senior advocate influence does not seem to help the Court select the most deserving cases for review. Because of this, it might seem natural to conclude that it is a good idea to take away the influence of senior advocates. But we don't think so. Indeed, the first step toward fixing the problems with senior advocates' influence is to recognize that it is not going to disappear. Trying to get rid of it is a waste of time.

The power and influence of elite lawyers is an inevitable part of any legal system. It is not unique to India. In the United States, for example, it is widely recognized that a small number of elite lawyers and law firms argue an unusually large number of cases in the United States Supreme Court.[31] This is true, even though the United States Supreme Court is very different from the Supreme Court of India— it has fewer judges (only nine), receives fewer petitions (about 8000 per year), and issues far fewer judgments on fully argued cases (about eighty per year).[32]

This should not be surprising because there are good reasons why elite lawyers *should* have more influence and *should* argue more cases. As we've noted, senior advocates have extensive experience in the Supreme Court (more even than the judges of the Supreme Court), and this experience corresponds to skill in legal matters. The most skilled advocates *should* be spending their time arguing to the Supreme Court.

Further, it is not clear how reforms could reduce the influence of senior advocates, even if doing so was a desirable goal. There is nothing in the formal rules of the Supreme Court that gives senior advocates an advantage. The judges themselves may not even realize that they favour petitions brought by senior advocates. Our evidence is consistent with an entirely unconscious bias toward senior advocates. Senior advocates will always have extensive experience with the Supreme Court and legal expertise and thus, they will command the respect of the judges before whom they argue. Of course, this does not mean that the power of senior advocates is a good thing. Given the high fees that senior advocates charge, it is usually only the rich who can afford their services. This puts the poor at a disadvantage, regardless of the merits of their cases.

The problem with senior advocates' influence is not solved by attempting to take away their influence. Rather, the problem is solved by ensuring that the power of senior advocates is directed toward beneficial ends. We turn to this next.

Focus on Senior Advocates' Legal Expertise

Precisely because senior advocates are influential, the success of any reforms in the Supreme Court will depend on their support. If senior advocates oppose the reforms, they won't happen. If senior advocates counteract the reforms, they will be ineffective. But if senior advocates embrace (or at least accept) the reforms, their clout with the Court will ensure that the reforms can succeed. Thus, just as petitioners to the Supreme Court want senior advocates to argue for them, a reformer seeking to strengthen the Court, improve the law and reduce delay, wants senior advocates as allies in the reform effort.

But why would senior advocates support change when the *status quo* is so good for them? Currently, senior advocates have unmatched influence and earn huge fees. They are likely to be happy with the system as it is.

To be attractive to senior advocates, a reform should not threaten their power and wealth. Fortunately, there is no need for reforms that reduce their importance to the Court. Instead, reforms can focus on trading one source of senior advocates' influence for another. Currently, senior advocates are valuable because, in a two-minute hearing, the judges have little basis for making an informed decision. When they see a senior advocate, they can defer to someone who is experienced and respected. This allows the Court to process hundreds of SLPs per day, but it doesn't help the Court reduce the crushing numbers of SLPs being filed or generate clear and consistent legal judgments.

Senior advocates are valuable for another reason, one that is currently underutilized. They are legal experts with deep knowledge of Supreme Court litigation. The irony of the *status quo* is that a large part of this expertise is wasted at admissions hearings. The hearings are too short for a lawyer to truly educate the judges about the relevant law and the importance of the legal issues to the Court. Court reforms that made legal expertise and experience in the Supreme Court more valuable would ensure that senior advocates would continue to be influential counsellors to the Court.

Thus, we see reform as a win-win opportunity for senior advocates and for the Court, so long as reforms focus on rewarding senior advocates' legal expertise rather than their 'face value'. Senior advocates would retain their esteemed position in the profession, but their influence would be channelled toward improving the quality of the Court's judgments, rather than giving the Court a quick way of sorting through petitions at admissions hearings.

We now turn to specific reforms that will accomplish this goal.

Create Rules that Reward Legal Expertise, not Prestige

Reforming the influence of senior advocates is not merely about correcting the unnecessary influence of a few powerful lawyers. It has a broader purpose, too.

As we have argued throughout this book, the Supreme Court would benefit from a greater focus on issuing judgments that announce clear legal rules. These court judgments should be based on past precedent and should be followed in future Supreme Court cases. Of course, writing hundreds of judgments per year and researching each one so that the Supreme Court applies rules consistently is a major challenge. But the judges do not have to do the work alone. The role of arguing the law and advising the Court is one senior advocates are meant to fill. It is only because of the Court's overwhelming caseload that so much of the work of senior advocates is devoted to face time at two-minute admissions hearings, rather than extensive legal research and argumentation.

Thus, reforming the role of the senior advocate is less about creating a new role for senior advocates than it is about returning senior advocates to their intended and best role.

The fact remains that the Court faces tens of thousands of SLPs competing for admission. This flood of petitions forces the Court to make snap decisions on SLPs, and the Court relies on senior advocates' face value to choose which ones to admit. Changing the role of senior advocates requires changing the conditions that lead to the heavy reliance on senior advocates at admissions hearings. First, reforms should reduce the number of SLPs. By cutting the flow of SLPs, the Court can make admissions decisions based on better grounds than the prestige of the lawyer who appears. Second, reforms should reduce the 'face value' of senior advocates in the eyes of judges. By reducing the gap in seniority and experience between senior advocates and judges, the relationship between judges and senior advocates can depend more on the senior advocates' value as legal experts and less on their status as the oldest and most experienced people in the room.

To achieve these goals, we propose two specific reforms:

- Create rules to admit only SLPs that raise important questions of law
- Raise the retirement age for Supreme Court judges.

Admit Only SLPs that Raise Important Questions of Law

As discussed in Chapter 2, to reduce the burden of sorting through more than 60,000 SLPs per year, the Court must take steps to reduce the number of petitions that are filed and to efficiently sort through the ones that are filed. One reform can accomplish both of these goals: The Court should create clear rules that allow admission only for those SLPs that raise important questions of law. In other words, to be admitted for a full hearing, an SLP should demonstrate to the Court that it raises an important question of law for which the courts of India require guidance from the Supreme Court.

Why will this ease the burden on the Court? First, fewer SLPs will be filed. Today, the Court's all-things-considered approach to admitting SLPs encourages parties to file SLPs because any argument that might attract the sympathy of the judges could be a winning argument. And in fact, many of the cases that attract the attention of the Court are not cases that raise interesting, important or difficult legal questions.

Indeed, as we have shown in Chapter 1, many of them raise no legal issues at all! When the rules for admitting SLPs are stated clearly in advance, anyone who fails to meet those criteria will think twice before filing.

Second, the judges of the Court will be able to make decisions to admit or dismiss SLPs more easily. Advocates and judges alike can focus their attention on a single question, 'Do the Indian courts need the Supreme Court to provide an answer to this question of law?' This question is the right question to ask for three reasons: (1) It ensures that the Supreme Court is admitting petitions that help all of the courts of India. (2) It clearly rules out many petitions unworthy of review, and thus reduces SLP filings. (3) It is a question that suits the expertise of senior advocates and Supreme Court judges.

To be sure, this reform will require the Supreme Court to reverse course. In 2016, a Constitution Bench of the Supreme Court expressly declined to specify guidelines for admitting SLPs.[33] But this change, of course, will not only relieve the flood of petitions the Court faces. Focusing on hearing petitions that raise legal issues of value to the court system will allow the Court to give clear guidance to the hundreds of courts that hear the millions of cases pending in India that the Supreme Court never directly sees. Further, with fewer petitioners filing SLPs, the Court will be able to devote more time to each case. More time allows for greater development of legal arguments—and less reliance on the prestige of the senior advocate.

Return to the story at the beginning of this Chapter—when a judge asks counsel, 'Is there any merit in your case?' the answer should not be, 'Your lordship, I flew all the way from the UK to appear at this hearing', should it?

Raise the Retirement Age of Supreme Court Judges

The other reform we propose requires legislative action. Mandatory retirement for Supreme Court judges at age sixty-five all but ensures that judges of the Supreme Court will spend no more than ten years on the Court, and usually much less. Senior advocates, in contrast, get decades of experience in the Supreme Court over the course of their careers. At age sixty-five, when judges of the Supreme Court are retiring, senior advocates are in their prime, with many years of practice ahead of them. With their advantage in seniority and experience over the judges, it is no wonder that senior advocates wield so much influence.

There is no reason that the law governing the tenure of Supreme Court judges should require this imbalance between the judges and the lawyers who argue before them. Indeed, a retirement age of sixty-five is unusually low when compared to judiciaries in other countries. As we show in Chapter 5, many countries have mandatory retirement at age seventy for judges.

Raising the retirement age for Supreme Court judges will counteract the undue influence of senior advocates. Judges will have longer tenures in the Supreme Court. They will have more experience on the Court and will not be as dependent on the experience of senior advocates. Of course, judges will still be reliant on senior advocates for legal arguments and authorities—but of course, that is as it should be.

This is not the only benefit of raising the retirement age of Supreme Court judges. As we show in Chapter 5, the early age at which Supreme Court judges must retire creates other problems, too.

Conclusion

Prior studies have shown that senior advocates have a greater success rate in getting petitions admitted at the Supreme Court as compared to non-senior advocates. Our study of a different dataset confirms this finding. We went further and examined the success rate of senior advocates in the final decision of the Court. We found conflicting results. In one set of data we examined, we found higher win rates for senior advocates than non-senior advocates. Using another dataset found non-senior advocates have a slightly higher win rate. Combined with the fact that judges spend just over one minute on a typical admissions hearing, our analysis suggests that judges are influenced by the reputation of the senior advocates in admitting cases.

Senior advocates are an elite group of lawyers (compromising less than 1 per cent of the Supreme Court lawyers). Their power can be used to help the Court make better admissions decisions. They can assist the Court in identifying cases that will provide better guidance to lower courts and make new rules rather than those that simply advance the cause of the client of the senior advocate. Policy suggestions we raised in other chapters will also have potential benefits for the role of senior advocates. Creating better guidelines for SLP admissions will give senior advocates more incentive to also identify cases that will have greater systemic impact. Increasing the retirement age of judges might also mean that judges will in the future have more seniority than they did in the past, thereby potentially reducing the need to rely on the reputation of the senior advocate in making admissions decisions.

4

First Amongst Equals? Master of the Roster and Strategic Case Assignments

An Extraordinary Press Conference

The bright crisp Friday morning of 12 January 2018 was devoted to admitting new matters at the Supreme Court. Lawyers and litigants thronged the premises of the Court, vying to convince the judges that their cases deserved to be taken up for a full hearing. Mid-morning, word started coming in that an 'extraordinary event' in the annals of the Indian judiciary was about to take place. The four senior-most judges of the Supreme Court after the Chief Justice of India were going to hold a press conference. For a tradition-and-precedent-bound institution, such a press conference was entirely unprecedented. Judges tend to be reticent and avoid the public eye—they let their judgments speak for themselves. Never before had Supreme Court judges come out to hold a press conference of this sort.

Justices Jasti Chelameswar, Ranjan Gogoi, Madan Lokur and Kurian Joseph sat on the lawns of Justice Chelameswar's house and addressed the media. They were concerned that 'many things that are less than desirable have happened in the last few months', such that 'democracy will not survive in this country' unless remedial action was taken.[1] What had brought on this concern? 'The assignment of a case,' said the judges.[2] They released a letter that they had written to the Chief Justice of India, Justice Dipak Misra, raising similar concerns and complaining that '[t]here have been instances where cases having far-reaching consequences for the nation and the institution have been assigned by the Chief Justice of this court selectively to the benches "of their preference" without any rational basis for such assignment.'[3] The implication was that the Chief Justice of India was using his position as the 'Master of the Roster' to influence judicial outcomes.

As the four judges recognized in their letter, the Chief Justice of India is the 'Master of the Roster'. This implies that the Chief Justice, and the Chief Justice alone, has the power to 'constitute the Benches of the Court and allocate cases to the Benches so constituted'.[4] Judges can only hear matters assigned to them by the Chief Justice or under his directions.[5]

As the Court has stated repeatedly, on the judicial side the Chief Justice is *primus inter pares*—first amongst equals.[6] That is, his vote counts only as much as the vote of other judges, no more, no less, and he has no greater say than other judges on judicial matters.[7] He is first only by virtue of being the senior-most.[8] However, on the administrative side, the Chief Justice exercises a range of powers as the head of the institution, the Master of the Roster power being one of them.

For routine matters, cases are assigned to two-judge benches on a subject-wise roster. That is, the Chief Justice decides, for example, that a two-judge bench of specified judges will hear all labour matters. The registry will then assign all labour matters to that bench. This type of rostering is subject-wise and not case specific. A fallout of the press conference was that this type of rostering, which was earlier not disclosed publicly, is now made available on the Supreme Court website.[9]

Apart from subject-wise rostering, the Chief Justice is sometimes called upon to constitute larger benches of three or more judges to resolve conflicting precedent or when a previous decision of the Court is in doubt;[10] or of five or more judges to hear substantial questions as to the interpretation of the Constitution or for certain other types of cases (these benches of five or more judges are called 'Constitution

Benches').[11] Here, the Chief Justice is required to constitute a specific bench and assign a particular case to that bench. This is the case-specific rostering power.[12]

The judges' press conference brought out into the open a simmering discontent with the exercise of the Master of the Roster powers by the then Chief Justice of India, Justice Dipak Misra. Just a few months prior to the press conference, a two-judge bench headed by Justice Jasti Chelameswar heard a matter pertaining to judicial corruption, in which the Chief Justice of India was potentially an interested party.[13] Since the case involved 'allegations which are disturbing . . . [and] pertain to the functioning of [the] Court',[14] the bench directed that the matter should be heard by a bench comprising the five senior-most judges of the Supreme Court. In effect, Justice Chelameswar determined the composition of the bench, possibly on the understanding that if the Chief Justice of India is an interested party, he should not be exercising the administrative power of bench allocation in the matter. A five-judge bench headed by the Chief Justice of India took exception to this usurpation of the Master of the Roster power by the two-judge bench, and reiterated that the power was reposed in the Chief Justice *alone*.[15]

This position was reiterated a few months after the press conference by the Court in two different cases where petitioners had challenged the Chief Justice's Master of the Roster power. In both cases, petitioners were concerned that there are no constraints—institutional or principled—on the exercise of the Master of the Roster power, which gives the Chief Justice enormous powers to influence judicial outcomes by assigning cases to particular judges. In the first case, the petitioner, Asok Pande, sought the creation of a 'set procedure' for constituting three- and five-judge benches.[16] In the second case, senior Advocate and former Law Minister, Shanti Bhushan, sought a declaration that the Master of the Roster power rests not in the Chief Justice alone, but in the 'collegium' of the senior-most judges of the Court (who are also responsible for judicial appointments).[17] Dismissing both petitioners, the Court reiterated the absolute power of the Chief Justice over the roster.

The Master of the Roster power, especially the power to assign particular cases to particular judges, gives the Chief Justice enormous power to control judicial outcomes. One might think that judges only apply law to the facts of the case and determine the outcome of the case accordingly. If that is the case, then who the judge is, makes little difference to the outcome of the case. However, this understanding of the process of adjudication stands debunked today. Who the judge is, her personal ideology, background and training, all influence judicial outcomes. This is because legal rules are often broadly worded and provide ample discretion to judges to determine the meaning of the rule. Added to this, judges have to decide which legal rules apply to the facts of the case, what are the established and relevant facts of the case, what do such facts demonstrate, and how do the rules as interpreted by the judge, apply to the facts s/he deems pertinent. This is why, particularly in controversial cases, judges often disagree with each other on what the right outcome should be. Such disagreement would rarely be possible if judicial decision making was a completely objective exercise.

If who the judge is impacts judicial outcomes, then the Chief Justice's power to assign specific cases to particular judges allows her to influence judicial outcomes in those cases. Absent any guidelines on how the Chief Justice exercises this power, there is little accountability for allocation of cases to judges. This was the concern raised in the petitions challenging the Master of the Roster power. And it was this concern of misuse of the power by the Chief Justice to achieve preferred outcomes, that was voiced by the four judges at the press conference.

Strategic Assignments—An ongoing concern

The concern about the strategic exercise of the Master of the Roster power by the Chief Justice to influence judicial outcomes is not new, but has grown over time. When the Supreme Court was first set up in 1950, the Court had eight seats (including the Chief Justice). Judges often sat together or in large benches and thus, the Chief Justice had little choice in the assignment of cases.[18] However, as the workload of the Court grew, so did the number of judges.[19] At the same time, bench sizes started getting smaller. The number of large benches constituted each year dwindled, from an average of seventy-one Constitution Benches per year in the first twenty-five years of the Court to only eleven such benches per year on average, thereafter.[20] Having a larger pool of judges to assign to smaller benches has meant that the Chief Justice now has greater discretion in case allocation. In the remainder of this chapter, we look at what the data reveals on how Chief Justices have deployed the Master of the Roster power.[21]

By 1974, George Gadbois was already observing a 'Chief Justice effect' on judicial outcomes.[22] Gadbois studied decisions between 1950 and 1967, a period covering the tenures of nine Chief Justices: Harilal Kania, M. Patanjali Sastri, Mehr Chand Mahajan, B. K. Mukherjea, Sudhi Ranjan Das, B. P. Sinha, P. B. Gajendragadkar, A. K. Sarkar and K. Subba Rao. Looking at cases that involved civil litigation between the government and an individual, he noted that each of these judges had widely varying rates of deciding in favour of the individual and against the government. This was especially true for split decisions—that is, decisions where all judges could not agree on the outcome. Between 1950 and 1967, the individual claimant won against the government in 39.6 per cent of all cases involving disputes between the two. In his entire tenure as a judge of the Supreme Court, Justice Subba Rao, for example, decided in favour of the individual 54.1 per cent of the time and in split decisions sided with the individual in 82.4 per cent of the cases. On the other hand, Justice Kania decided in favour of the individual in only 24.2 per cent of the cases in all decisions and 22.2 per cent of cases involving a split decision. The other seven judges fell somewhere in between. During Justice Subba Rao's tenure as Chief Justice, the Supreme Court as a whole decided in favour of the individual and against the government in 49.7 per cent of cases involving disputes between the two. On the other hand, during his tenure as the Chief Justice, Justice Kania's Supreme Court decided in favour of the individual and against the government only 32.7 per cent of the time. Gadbois found a positive, though not statistically significant correlation between a Chief Justice's own decision-making pattern during his tenure as a judge of the Court, and the decision-making pattern of the Supreme Court during his tenure as Chief

Justice. That is, the more likely a Chief Justice was to decide in favour of the individual (and against the government), the more likely the Supreme Court was, during the tenure of that Chief Justice, to decide in favour of the individual.

Gadbois' data and analysis indicate that the Chief Justice's power to assign cases to benches can and does influence outcomes of cases, though Chief Justices cannot completely control outcomes since they cannot generally control or know for certain how other judges will decide cases. Some Chief Justices are more likely to use their power to construct benches that will suit their preferred outcomes, others will not. Perhaps the most obvious example of a Chief Justice's impact on case outcomes is that of Justice Subba Rao. In his time, Justice Subba Rao had authored the largest number of dissents on the Supreme Court up to that point—forty-eight dissents in 466 cases of which he was part, at a dissent rate of 10.3 per cent. However, once he became the Chief Justice, he was *never* in dissent in even a single one of the seventy-seven cases that he participated in. Crucially, sixteen of these cases involved a split decision, so there were at least two views on the bench on how the case should be decided. However, Justice Subba Rao was always in the majority.[23] Gadbois later recounted that, in a meeting he had with Justice Subba Rao, the latter admitted to stacking the benches in his favour once he was the Chief Justice of India.[24]

Justice Subba Rao was not alone in never being on the losing side of an argument as a Chief Justice. Of the nine Chief Justices that Gadbois studied, only three were ever in the minority in a split decision. Many of the judges that Gadbois interviewed during the 1980s openly admitted or agreed that many Chief Justices strategically assigned benches in order to impact outcomes.[25]

Similar patterns continue to the present day. Nick Robinson found between 1950 and 2009, the Chief Justice had been in dissent in only ten out of 1532 Constitution Bench cases dealing with constitutional issues, at a dissent rate of 0.7 per cent.[26] Compare this to an overall dissent rate of 15 per cent in these 1532 decisions. In our own study of cases decided by the Supreme Court between 2010 and 2015, out of thirty-nine cases decided by a Constitution Bench, we found that the Chief Justice was *never* in dissent. By itself, this might not be remarkable if judges rarely dissent. It is true that the overall rate of dissent in Supreme Court cases is very low. In the time period of our study, dissents occurred in only 0.5 per cent of the cases overall. This number goes up once we look only at three-judge and larger benches. Cases decided by three-judge benches were 3.5 times (1.8 per cent) more likely to feature a dissent as compared to the overall average. Constitution Bench cases of five or more judges, were twelve times (5.9 per cent) more likely than average to have a dissenting opinion.[27] This is not surprising. Larger benches deal with more controversial or unsettled issues, and are therefore more likely to result in a lack of consensus. Further, as has been empirically proven in other jurisdictions, the larger the number of judges, the more likely it is that there will be a difference of opinion.[28] However, what is surprising is that the Chief Justice, who overall dissented at the same rate as other judges on smaller benches,[29] *never* dissented on the Constitution Bench. Even though other judges were on average likely to dissent twelve times more on Constitution Benches as compared to their overall dissent rate, for the Chief Justice, the dissent rate dropped to zero on Constitution Benches. That is, the Chief Justice was *always* on the winning side of a split decision on a Constitution Bench.

Interestingly, there were more dissents on benches headed by the Chief Justice than on benches where the Chief Justice was not present.[30] On the face of it, this might suggest that the Chief Justice does not engage in strategic case assignments. However, given that the Chief Justice, unlike all other judges, is never in the minority, a more likely explanation is that the Chief Justice assigns himself to the most controversial cases, which are more likely to see dissents.[31] This might not be concerning if Chief Justices follow a 'seniority' norm in assigning such cases so that the senior-most judges hear the most controversial cases. The complaint of the judges at the press conference was that very important matters were being decided by relatively 'junior' judges. The implication was that the norm was for important matters to be decided by 'senior' judges, and that this norm was being flouted. Using larger bench size as a rough proxy for the importance of a matter, we examined whether judges are assigned to these benches by seniority. However, on running regressions on bench assignment *vis a vis* seniority of judges based on their date of appointment to the Supreme Court, we found that there is no correlation between seniority of a judge and their likelihood to be assigned to a three-judge or a Constitution Bench.[32]

Even though other judges are not assigned to three-judge or larger benches on the basis of seniority, this has not prevented the Chief Justice from over-assigning cases to himself. Our data shows that the Chief Justice is 3.6 times as likely to be on a three-judge bench as compared to the next senior most judge.[33] Nick Robinson found that between 1950 and 2009, the Chief Justice sat on 77 per cent of Constitution Benches.[34] In the cases covered in our study, Chief Justices assigned 88 per cent of the Constitution Bench cases to themselves, and were four times more likely to be on a Constitution Bench as the next senior-most judge.[35] On average, a judge had a roughly one in five chance (18.3 per cent) of sitting on a Constitution Bench and the median judge had a 1 in 8 chance (13 per cent) of sitting on a Constitution Bench. The Chief Justice, on the other hand, has an approximate one in 1.14 chance (88 per cent) of sitting on a Constitution Bench.

In a system of random allocation to Constitution Benches, such as by lottery, we would expect that all judges, including the Chief Justice, would be assigned to a Constitution Bench in roughly equal numbers. Clearly, the Chief Justice is over-represented in Constitution Bench decisions, and the allocation is not taking place completely randomly. As discussed above, the allocation to three-judge benches is also not on the basis of seniority.

What, then, is the basis for the assignment of judges to larger benches? The concern voiced at the press conference and generally by court watchers is that Chief Justices may be using the Master of the Roster power to allocate judges to specific cases in such a way as to influence outcomes in those cases.[36] A Chief Justice cannot (one would hope) be entirely certain *ex ante* how judges on a bench are going to decide cases. For that reason, Chief Justices cannot completely control outcomes. However, they may manipulate bench composition in ways that are more likely to suit their preferred outcomes. As discussed above,

Gadbois' work has already indicated that who the Chief Justice is, does tend to influence judicial outcomes, even on benches that the Chief Justice is not part of. His study also found that judges who were more inclined to dissent were frozen out of Constitution Benches, perhaps in order to exclude 'mavericks' who could upset the predictability of outcomes. In our own study we found that nearly a third of the judges (32 per cent, or eighteen out of fifty-seven judges)[37] were never assigned to a Constitution Bench, despite having on average twenty-two Constitution Benches available for assignment during their tenure on the bench.

We also found that although Chief Justices assign themselves to many Constitution Benches, they give this special treatment only to themselves. Judges in line to become Chief Justice get no special treatment. Perhaps the most startling example of this is Justice T. S. Thakur, himself in line to become the Chief Justice, who was not assigned to any of the fifty-eight Constitution Benches constituted by his immediate six predecessors. Likewise, for Justice Altamas Kabir, his immediate two predecessors assigned him to one out of sixteen and one out of fourteen cases each. Justice H. L. Dattu was assigned to two out of thirteen Constitution Benches by his immediate predecessor, but one out of forty-two by the previous four cumulatively.

Another trend noticeable in our study was that often Chief Justices tend to over-assign (in comparison to other judges) to Constitution Bench those judges who were appointed to the Supreme Court during their own Chief Justiceship. Recall that the Chief Justice heads the collegium that selects judges to the Supreme Court. Therefore, a judge appointed during the tenure of a particular Chief Justice most likely has the Chief Justice's approval and confidence, and is potentially not very divergent in ideology and policy preferences. Of the judges who were available for assignment to a Constitution Bench in the time period of our study, judges tended to be assigned on average to roughly a fifth (18.3 per cent) of the Constitution Benches constituted during their tenure on the Court. Compare this with Justice P. Sathasivam's record—he was elevated during the Chief Justiceship of Justice K. G. Balakrishnan and promptly assigned to fourteen out of the fifteen Constitution Benches assigned by Justice Balakrishnan after Justice Sathasivam's appointment to the Supreme Court. However, the succeeding Chief Justices assigned him to only one out of eighteen cases before he himself took over as Chief Justice. Justice J. S. Khehar's assignments also followed a similar trajectory—he was assigned to all the Constitution Benches set up by Chief Justice S. H. Kapadia who headed the collegium that appointed Justice Khehar. After this, Justices Kabir and Sathasivam did not assign Justice Khehar to any of the eight Constitution Benches during their tenures. Once Justice R. M. Lodha took over, Justice Khehar was again assigned to Constitution Benches. A similar trend of disproportionate assignments by the appointing Chief Justice, followed by a drop in assignments subsequently is seen with Justice M. Y. Eqbal (assigned to three out of three Constitution Benches by Justice Kabir); Justice Ranjana Desai (assigned to three out of four Constitution Benches by Justice Kapadia); Justice Rohinton F. Nariman (appointed to four out of seven benches by Justice Lodha); and Justice Vikramjeet Sen (appointed to two out of two benches by Justice Kabir but not appointed to any of the eighteen benches by the succeeding three Chief Justices). Recall that as newly appointed judges, these judges were on the junior end of the Supreme Court when they were appointed to Constitution Benches at rates much higher than the average, and were not appointed at similar rates thereafter. Since the Chief Justice heads the collegium that appoints judges to the Supreme Court, the trend observed here seems to suggest that Chief Justices are likely to appoint favoured junior judges to Constitution Benches. These numbers are too small to make a statistical evaluation possible, but they do point to the possibility of strategic assignments to Constitution Benches.

Similarly, some judges seem to get frozen out of Constitution Benches under some Chief Justices and are assigned to higher-than-average numbers under others. Take for example Justice K. S. Panicker Radhakrishnan who was appointed to nine out of fourteen Constitution Benches by Justice Kapadia, but to no other Constitution Benches by the succeeding three Chief Justices. Justice Ranjan Gogoi, one of the four judges who participated in the press conference, was himself assigned to Constitution Benches as a relatively junior judge by the first two Chief Justices that he served with (five out of twelve with Justices Kabir and Sathasivam cumulatively), but to none by the next two Chiefs (Justices Lodha and Dattu). Justice S. S. Nijjar found favour with Justices Kapadia (seven out of fourteen) and Kabir (two out of four), but not with the next two Chiefs, who did not assign him to any of the fourteen Constitution Benches between them. Clearly, in these cases, seniority did not play a role since these judges were frozen out of the Constitution Bench as they rose in seniority. Again, these numbers are too small for meaningful statistical examination, but they do point to the likelihood of non-random factors at play in assignment to Constitution Benches.

A study by Shrutanjaya Bharadwaj, who examined assignments to Constitution Benches between 2016 and 2019, confirms that the patterns that we observed in our study continued subsequently.[38] He also noted that of the thirty-nine Constitution cases between 2016 and 2019, the Chief Justice of India presided over thirty-two. He was in dissent in one case, making that the only Constitution Bench case in which a Chief Justice was in dissent in the seventy-eight Constitution Bench cases between 2010 and 2019.[39]

What do we have cumulatively? The Chief Justice has an untrammelled power to assign judges to Constitution Benches. If this power were being deployed in a completely random manner, as if by lottery, we would expect that every judge would have a roughly equal likelihood of being on a Constitution Bench. We would expect that the Chief Justice would be in majority or in dissent in split decisions consistent with the patterns and rates of dissent of other judges or with their own overall dissent rates. We find, however, that the assignment to larger benches, especially to constitutional benches is not random. Chief Justices over-assign themselves to Constitution Benches, while others are either completely frozen out or favoured for inclusion on Constitution Benches at disproportionate rates (disproportionate to assignment rates generally, and disproportionate to their own future trajectories). Further, while other judges dissent at higher rates on Constitution Benches, the Chief Justice is almost never in the minority on a Constitution Bench. This implies that such benches are constituted in a manner that the Chief Justice always carries the majority with him, a feat that no other judge can equal.

The disproportionate inclusion or exclusion of other judges also cannot be explained by considerations that are independent of who the judge is, such as seniority or status as a future Chief Justice. Previous studies have found that benches constituted by a Chief Justice were likely to favour outcomes consistent with the voting pattern of that Chief Justice, even when that Chief Justice was not himself on the bench. Judges were also frozen out of Constitution Benches to keep frequent dissenters who may upset the predictability of outcomes, at bay.

Taken together, this data suggests that assignments to Constitution Benches are strategic, and are consistent with the hypothesis that the Master of the Roster power is deployed with a view to influencing outcomes.

An Unaccountable Power

The judges who gave the press conference were concerned that there had been certain instances of strategic assignment by Chief Justice Dipak Misra 'without any rational basis for such assignment'.[40] This chapter demonstrates that the Master of the Roster controversy is not merely about, and should not be reduced to, individual instances. The Master of the Roster power presents a systemic problem for the judiciary in at least two ways. First, in principle, the power is untrammelled, and there is no clarity on the principles by which it is exercised. For this reason, there is little accountability for the exercise of the power, which leaves open the possibility of misuse in individual cases, and for strategic deployment to suit outcomes preferred by the Chief Justice more generally. Second, in practice, the rostering power is deployed in a strategic manner, across the board, and not only in discrete instances. So, when the Chief Justice over-assigns Constitution Bench cases to himself, this contradicts the claim that the Chief Justice has no more power than other judges on the judicial side. The Chief Justice wields the Master of the Roster power to give himself a greater say than other judges in shaping judicial discourse and in deciding the most important issues of the day. By constituting benches in a manner that the Chief Justice is never on the losing side of a split decision in a Constitution Bench, the Chief Justice is able to ensure his preferred outcomes, which is a power that no other judge has on the judicial side. Gadbois' work indicates that the Chief Justice has an influence on judicial outcomes—across the board—even on benches that the Chief Justice is not part of. It is a fallacy then to say that the Chief Justice is only *primus inter pares*. The Master of the Roster power has given the office of the Chief Justice primacy even in judicial decision-making.

From Trust to Accountability

The press conference was of limited success. In response to the concerns raised by the four judges, the subject-wise roster, that is, the subject-wise assignment of routine matters to specific benches, was made public. However, the power to assign specific cases to judges continued to be at the sole discretion of the Chief Justice, and this power was upheld by two subsequent judgments.[41] In the Parliament, an impeachment motion was moved against Chief Justice Dipak Misra for, amongst others reasons, 'abus[ing] his administrative authority as master of roster to arbitrarily assign individual cases of particular advocates in politically sensitive cases to select judges in order to achieve a predetermined outcome'.[42] The motion failed at the threshold when the Vice-President rejected the impeachment motion.[43] Ironically, when this rejection was challenged before the Supreme Court, Justice Dipak Misra himself constituted a five-judge bench to hear the matter.[44] Justice Ranjan Gogoi, one of the four judges who held the press conference, succeeded Justice Misra as the Chief Justice of India in October 2018. Here was an opportunity for him to place constraints on the Master of the Roster power. He failed spectacularly. If anything, he deployed the power even more controversially, to constitute and assign himself to a bench to hear a matter pertaining to an allegation of sexual harassment against him.[45] Other bench assignments during his tenure also raised questions about the misuse of the power.[46] The controversy lives on.

What can be done? The Master of the Roster power cannot be wished away. Courts need some mechanism or person to decide which judge is going to hear what cases. Given the unpredictability of schedules and circumstances, some person or body has to take calls and exercise some discretion in assigning cases. This is why multi-panel courts around the world struggle with the problem of assigning cases to judges and benches in a way that secures orderly functioning but does not bias outcomes.[47]

How then can the exercise of this power be constrained to limit its arbitrary or strategic exercise? In the two cases on this issue that were filed before the Supreme Court, the Court exhorted petitioners (and the public at large) to trust that the Chief Justice of India, who occupies a 'high constitutional office',[48] will follow the 'path of rectitude',[49] and exercise the Master of the Roster power fairly. As this chapter has shown, this trust is misplaced. More importantly, as a public functionary exercising immense public power in a democratic system, the Chief Justice of India's actions cannot be taken on trust alone. In a democratic system, trust is founded on transparency and accountability in the exercise of power, not on unquestioning faith in powerful individuals.

The norms and mechanisms by which administrative law holds public power to account in a democracy can guide us in designing a more accountable case allocation system. One solution for addressing the problem of strategic assignments by the Chief Justice is to remove discretion from the Chief Justice and automate assignments through mechanisms such as computerized allocations. This approach has been advocated in India as well.[50] A version of this approach is already in place for regular assignments to two-judge benches. Another oft-advocated approach to curtail the Chief Justice's discretion is to constitute one or more 'permanent Constitution Benches', that hear all pending matters without the need for case-specific assignments.[51] Both these approaches will significantly curtail the Chief Justice's discretionary Master of the Roster power. A permanent Constitution Bench will also make it difficult for the Chief Justice to evade deciding controversial cases by simply not setting up a bench at all.[52]

However, by itself, removing discretion will not address the many complications that come with administering a multi-panel court. For example, the need for discretion will persist in deciding whom to appoint to these permanent benches. This is especially important since the Chief Justice will have some idea of the nature of cases that a Constitution Bench is likely to hear in the near future and could still engage in strategic allocations. Further, scheduling conflicts, conflicts of interest resulting in judges recusing themselves and being ill or otherwise unavailable, all require intervention and override of automated decisions. So also, larger benches of seven or more judges may be required in rare instances, and these cannot be set up in advance. And finally, automation and algorithms shift the sites and modalities of how discretion is exercised but do not do away with the need for decisions. They can encode bias in their formulation that hides behind a veneer of 'technological impartiality'.[53]

Hence, the need to exercise discretion will persist despite efforts to automate or otherwise restrict discretion. An additional approach then is constraining this discretion by ensuring transparency and accountability for its exercise. Two suggestions along these lines were made in cases that came up before the Supreme Court on the Chief Justice's Master of the Roster power. In *Shanti Bhushan v. Supreme Court of India*,[54] petitioners advocated putting in place institutional mechanisms to constrain the power of the Chief Justice. They argued that the rostering power should lie with the collegium and not with the Chief Justice alone. However, as the Court rightly pointed out, this approach is likely to be impractical because the collegium does not meet every day whereas rostering needs arise on a daily basis. For example, when judges recuse themselves from a case, the case has to be marked to a different bench. These kinds of issues arise routinely, often daily, and require the Master of the Roster to exercise discretion. A collegium-level body for exercising the Master of the Roster powers may therefore be unworkable or at the very least unwieldy and inefficient.

In *Asok Pande v. Supreme Court of India*,[55] the petitioner argued for putting in place norms and procedures that guide the assignment of cases. Establishing norms for the exercise of discretion can both constrain discretion and provide standards by which to hold its exercise accountable. In the present context, such norms would guide the Chief Justice in exercising discretion in those situations where the automation of the decision is not enough. To account for unforeseen circumstances, the Chief Justice's power to override the norms would have to be preserved. However, by requiring justification in writing—and hence transparency—for departures from the established norms, the override or exceptions power will hopefully not swallow the rule. For example, hypothetically, if the general norm for allocations is based on the seniority of judges,[56] then as a general rule, the senior-most judges should be assigned to Constitution Benches. However, if for reasons such as a conflict of interest a judge has to recuse themselves, then the next senior-most judge should be inducted onto the bench. Any override or departure from the general norm, should require reasons in writing from the Chief Justice to ensure that the exercise of discretion is transparent and based on sound reasons. On the judicial side, the Court imposes similar requirements of transparency, fairness, and principled reasons for action, for imposing accountability on administrators in exercising public power. Returning the Chief Justice's Master of the Roster power to its proper place as an accountable administrative device is critical to ensuring that the Chief Justice of India truly remains no more than *primus inter pares*.

5

People Like Us: Diversity (or Lack Thereof) in Judicial Appointments

A unique feature of the Indian judicial system is that Supreme Court judges effectively appoint other Supreme Court judges. The body that is responsible for judicial appointments is called the collegium, which consists of the Chief Justice of India and the four most senior judges on the Supreme Court at any given time. The collegium recommends candidates to become judges of the Supreme Court and also has an important role in high court appointments. Unlike most of the other countries in the world, the executive does not play a role in the nomination process.

The collegium sends the President a list of the names of the people they wish to nominate as judges and the President ususally approves the list. Although the President has the power to send back a candidate that the collegium chooses, she is required to accept the nomination of the candidate if the collegium unanimously repeats its request. It should be noted that under the Modi adminstration, the executive has been more aggressive in refusing to move the collegium's nominations forward as compared to prior administrations.

Frustrated that neither the executive nor the Parliament play a meaninful role in the appointments of judges to the highest court of the country, in 2014 the Parliament passed a constitutional amendment that changed the process of appointments, giving the power to a commission consisting of a wide array of different stakeholders.[1] This would have brought India in line with 80 per cent of commonwealth countries, which have also created a commission for judicial appointments.[2]

In a remarkable move, the Indian Supreme Court struck down this constitutional amendment in 2015. The Court argued that judicial independence would be compromised if the executive branch of government was involved in the appointment of judges.

Judges did not always appoint other judges in India. In this chapter, we explain how and why an executive-led judicial appointment system became a judiciary-led system. We also discuss the various critques leveled against the existing system of appointments to the Supreme Court. We focus on one particular critique—whether or not the judges represent India's diversity. A judiciary that is diverse will gain more legitmacy and may also make better decisions. Our analysis of the appointments of the judges to the Supreme Court by the collegium demonstrate that the collegium has been far less concerned with gender and caste diversity than they are with religious and regional diversity. Our analysis also found that there has been no sigificant improvement over time in diversity of judges even as compared to the appointments made under the executive-led system that prevailed until 1993.[3]

An Executive-Led Appointments System Prevails (1950)

Article 124 of the Constitution of India states that '[e]very judge of the Supreme Court shall be appointed by the President.' However, it further states that the President shall appoint judges '. . . after *consultation* with such of the Judges of the Supreme Court and of High Courts in the States as the President may deem necessary'. (emphasis added). It further states that 'in the case of appointment of a Judge other than the Chief Justice, the Chief Justice of India shall always be consulted.'[4]

All of the major actors in early post-independence India interpreted this provision to mean that the Chief Justice of India would provide input and advice to the President, but the President was not bound by the advice of the Chief Justice or any other judge. In practice, the candidates were appointed only if the Chief Justice consented. But in many cases, the Chief Justice would withdraw his nomination if he realized that the candidate would not be approved.[5] The Chief Justice would propose candidates to the President and if the President rejected the candidate, a new person would be proposed until an agreeable candidate was found.

A practice that crystalized during the early days of the Indian democracy was that the judge who became the Chief Justice would be the judge that was most senior on the Court. Senority is determined by the date of appointment to the Supreme Court. In 1951, after Justice H.J. Kania, the first Chief Justice of India, died, the executive attempted to appoint a judge to the post of Chief Justice who was not the most senior judge.[6] All of the members of the Court at the time threatened to resign. As a result, Prime Minister Nehru backed down and appointed the judge with the appropriate seniority.

The seniority norm was then followed by the government until Prime Minister Indira Gandhi boldly deviated from it. Angered by the *Kesavananda Bharati* decision, in which the Court gave itself the power to invalidate constitutional amendments, she appointed Justice A.N. Ray to the position of Chief Justice in 1973.[7] In so doing, she skipped over three other judges more senior to him who had joined the majority position in *Kesavananda Bharati* while Justice Ray had dissented in the case.

Then again, when Indira Gandhi imposed the Emergency (1975–77), during which the operation of constitutionally guaranteed fundamental rights were suspended, she used judicial appointments as a way to reward justices who supported her point of view in cases. In the *ADM Japalpur* judgment, the Supreme Court in agreement with the executive, found that certain protections against arbitrary detention such as the writ of *habeas corpus* were not available during the Emergency.[8] The lone dissenting judge in that case, Justice H.R. Khanna, was passed over for the Chief Justiceship in favour of a more junior judge.[9] Prime Minister Indira Gandhi's attempts to subvert the independence of the judiciary—by giving judges incentives to side with the government—inform much of the national discussion on judicial appointments today.

The Collegium is Created (1993)

It is against the backdrop of this historical contestation between the executive and the judicary over judicial appointments that the first challenge to the executive-led appointments system was brought to the Supreme Court in 1981. The petitioners were lawyers who were challenging the transfer of various high court judges to different courts. The questions the Supreme Court addressed in that case related both to the appointment of high court judges and Supreme Court judges. Known today as the *First Judges Case* (*S.P. Gupta v. Union of India*),[10] the petitioners argued that the word 'consultation' in the relevant provisions of the Constitution should be read as 'concurrence' and that the judiciary should exercise a veto over judicial appointments.[11] The challenge failed and the Court held that in the event of a disagreement between the executive and the Chief Justice on whom to appoint as a judge of the Supreme Court, the views of the executive would prevail.[12]

Article 217 of the Constitution of India also states that high court judges should be appointed by the President in 'consultation' with the Chief Justice of India, the governor of the state, and in the case of an appointment of a judge other than the Chief Justice, the Chief Justice of the high court.[13] Here again, the Court concluded in the *First Judges* case that if there is a disagreement between the decision-makers, the views of the executive would prevail in appointments.[14]

After the *First Judges Case* was decided, Prime Minister Rajiv Gandhi's government was accused of its own court-packing scheme. The government would appoint only acting Chief Justices to high courts until those justices confirmed the government's nominees to the high courts.[15] Corruption charges were leveled against the judiciary and impeachment proceedings were brought in Parliament against a former Chief Justice.[16] In 1993, with these events fresh on everyone's minds, nine judges of the Supreme Court decided the *Second Judges Case* (*Supreme Court Advocates on Record Association v.*

Union of India).[17] The petitioners in the *Second Judges Case* brought virtually the same arguments against the executive-led appointments system to the Court as were raised in the *First Judges Case*. This time, the Court decided that the executive was abusing its powers and not giving enough consideration to merit when nominating judges to the Supreme Court. Even though the Constitution states that the Chief Justice must be 'consulted' in appointment decisions, the Supreme Court found that the Chief Justice must 'concur' in any appointments' decision, not just provide input.

In the *Second Judges Case*, the Court articulated a new appointment procedure. The Supreme Court called for the creation of a collegium. The collegium would consist of the Chief Justice and the two senior-most justices of the Court. In appointing persons to the high courts, the Collegium would consult with the senior-most Supreme Court judge hailing from the high court from which the candidate was to be appointed. The collegium would then propose the candidate to the executive. If the executive did not agree with the collegium's selection, the recommendation would be sent back. However, if the collegium reiterated its recommendation, the government would be bound to accept it.

The Court also discussed the basis on which the collegium should decide whom to appoint to the Supreme Court. It stated that the seniority of judges within their high court and across all courts should be the primary ground for appointment to the Supreme Court. However, other considerations such as outstanding merit and ensuring regional and other diversity, could be grounds to depart from the seniority norm.

In an advisory opinion issued in 1998 known as the *Third Judges Case*, the Supreme Court modified and further clarified the appointments system.[18] In it, the Court increased the number of judges in the collegium for the appointment of Supreme Court judges from the two senior-most to the four senior-most. The Court also held that the executive did not have to accept a nominee whose name is reiterated by the collegium unless the entire collegium is unanimous in its recommendation.

The Supreme Court Rejects A New Appointments Process Proposed By the Parliament (2015)

In 2014, a new government led by Prime Minister Narendra Modi came to power vowing to reform governmental institutions. Shortly after he rose to power, both houses of the Parliament as well as half the state legislatures passed the constitutional amendment that would create a judicial appointments' commission. The members of the commission were to be the Chief Justice of India, the two senior-most justices of the Supreme Court after the Chief Justice, the Union minister of law and justice and two eminent persons. The eminent persons would themselves be selected by a committee consisting of the prime minister, the leader of the Opposition in the lower house of the Parliament (the Lok Sabha) and the Chief Justice of India. At least one of the eminent persons had to be a member of a scheduled caste, scheduled tribe and other backward classes, or a minority or a woman.[19] The constitutional amendment provided that if two members of the commission voted against the appointment of a person, then the person would not be appointed.[20] This provision would later play an outsized role in the Supreme Court's judgment that rejected the commission as unconstitutional.

The constitutional amendment and statute were challenged before the Supreme Court in the *Fourth Judges Case* (*Supreme Court Advocates on Record Association v. Union of India*).[21] A five-judge bench of the Court struck down the amendment with one judge dissenting from the opinion. Every judge on the bench issued an opinion in the case, filling over 1042 pages. The Court grounded its decision (among other things) in its power to review amendments to the Constitution as well as acts of the Parliament under *Kesavananda Bharati v. State of Kerala*.[22] Under what is now known as the 'basic structure doctrine', the Court determines whether a constitutional amendment abrogates a feature of the Constitution that is so central to the Constitution's identity that the abrogation changes the very character of the Constitution.

In the *Fourth Judges Case*, the Court stated that 'judicial independence' is part of the basic structure of the Constitution that cannot be impeded by the Parliament. However, the Court then took an additional step by suggesting that the judiciary must have primacy in appointments of judges in order to ensure judicial independence.[23] One evidence for this conclusion is that the word 'consultation' in the appointments' clauses of the Constitution meant that the views of judges on appointments should be given primacy.[24]

The Court was concerned that the composition and voting procedures of the proposed commission meant that judges did not have the decisive authority on appointments. Two people could veto decisions even when the judges could sway another member of the commission.[25] Justice Khehar also opposed the role for any executive officer in selecting judges. Since the government is the largest litigant at the Court, he worried that the law minister would not be impartial.[26] Justice Lokur's opinion raised concerns that the new appointments' commission would impede the checks and balances of democracy.[27]

Many authors have criticized the *Fourth Judges Case* on several grounds. Some argue that the Court misinterpreted the drafting history and the debates that took place in the Constituent Assembly.[28] Another line of argument attacks the assumption that the primacy of judges in the appointments process is an unamendable feature of the Constitution.[29] Indeed, the lone dissenter, Justice Chelameswar, argued that there is no basis in constitutional history for the proposition that the primacy of the judiciary in appointments is a basic feature of the Constitution.[30] Justice Chelameswar also critiqued the argument that any involvement of the executive in the judicial appointments process contravenes the separation of powers.[31]

Another major shortcoming is the lack of any definition of the concept of judicial independence. The power of Supreme Court justices to appoint other judges in the higher judiciary is neither sufficient nor necessary to ensure judicial independence. It is not sufficient, because as we will show in Chapter 6, the need for post-retirement employment gives judges the incentive to cater to the government when deciding cases. It is not necessary, because there are other ways to protect the indepedence of the judiciary—judges have the certainty of tenure, protection from removal from office, protection of salaries and immunity from scrutiny in the discharge of judicial duties except in the case of misconduct.[32]

At the same time, as they upheld the collegium, many of the judges admitted that the collegium needed reform. Accordingly, the Court held a 'consequential hearing', and asked for suggestions from the public on changes that should be made to the collegium system. While it ultimately left the decision of finalizing the procedure for the working of the collegium to the government in consultation with the collegium, the Court opined that the reform of the collegium should focus on specifying eligibility criteria for appointments, introducing a transparent process for decision-making, setting up a permanent secretariat to assist the collegium for better management of the appointments system and a mechanism to entertain complaints against those who are being considered for appointment, among other issues.[33]

Problems with Judges Appointing other Judges in Practice

Beyond the critiques of the substance and reasoning of the *Fourth Judges Cases* rejecting the proposal for a commission, many have observed a number of problems with the collegium system in practice. First, many people, including former Supreme Court justice Ruma Pal, have criticized the process for its lack of transparency.[34] Meetings of the collegium are conducted in secret and there is no indication as to why certain candidates are selected and others rejected for nomination. This lack of transparency and unchecked authority is questionable for a democratic polity. When he became a member of the collegium, Justice Chelameswar refused to attend its meetings.[35] He had earlier been the sole dissenter in the *Fourth Judges case*. After Justice Chelameswar's mini-revolt, in an effort to increase transparency in candidate selections, the Supreme Court's website began including the resolutions of the meetings of the collegium in 2017.[36] These resolutions were broadly worded and gave some indication as to why a person was being recommended for an appointment to the Supreme Court. However, although the practice continues the resolutions are fairly vague.[37]

Second, others argue that the selection of nominees is informed by corruption and favouritism.[38] Some worthy candidates are not put forward because of a personal animosity.[39] For example, one high court chief justice claimed he was not appointed to the Supreme Court because he did not appoint the sister of the Chief Justice of India to his high court.[40] To avoid this kind of politics, the collegium typically selects high court judges on the basis of their seniority but it also deviates from that norm when it wants to.

Third, the body that appoints judges to the Supreme Court and high courts, the collegium, has itself not represented the diveristy of India. Since the system was implemented in 1993, the collegium predominantly consists of upper caste men. Only two women have been part of the collegium—Justice Pal (2003–06) and Justice R. Banumathi (2019–20).[41] There have only been two scheduled caste members in the collegium—Justice Balakrishnan and Justice Sathasivam. The judicial commission that was proposed by the Parliament would have been more diverse than the collegium. One member of the commission would always have been a woman or a person belonging to a scheduled caste or scheduled tribe.[42]

The Importance of a Gender and Caste Diverse Judiciary

Ensuring that the judiciary is representative of the people in the country furthers a number of important values. Judges bring their own personal experiences to their decision-making, and having judges who come from different backgrounds can lead to better decisions.[43] Judiciaries that are representative of the people will be considered more legitimate and can count on greater trust and confidence from the public at large. Conversely, lack of diversity in judiciaries can undermine public confidence in the judicial process. Finally, a diverse judiciary is more likely to make better informed and impartial decisions. When judges appoint each other, there is likely an incentive to choose people with similar views.

Two forms of diversity that have garnered significant attention in the Indian democracy are gender and caste diversity. The need for greater representation of excluded genders and castes within public institutions is embedded in the Indian Constitution through provisions on affirmative action. Affirmative action is provided in the form of reservations or quotas in the legislature in local self-government, in government jobs and in education.

Over time, reservation categories have been broadened. The Socially and Educationally Backward Classes Commission, more popularly known as the Mandal Commission, issued a report in 1983 that called for the inclusion of another group of people—Other Backward Castes (OBCs)—in the reservation system for central government jobs. In 1990, the government moved to implement the report. As per the data available with the Mandal Commission, OBCs constitute nearly 52 per cent of the population.[44]

Reservations for women in political institutions have also been introduced in the last few decades. In 1992, the 73rd Amendment to the Constitution provided that one-third of the seats in local governments must be reserved for women. In 1993, a constitutional amendment was passed in India that called for one-third of village council leader positions in gram panchayat to be reserved for women. In addition, the Women's Reservation Bill or the Constitution (108th Amendment) Bill, 2008 proposes to amend the Constitution of India to reserve 33 per cent of all seats in the the Lok Sabha (the lower house of Parliament) and in all state legislative assemblies for women.[45] The seats were proposed to be reserved in rotation and would have been determined by draw of lots in such a way that a seat would be reserved only once in three consecutive general elections. After a long battle, the bill was passed by the Rajya Sabha (the upper house of the Parliament) in 2010. It still is awaiting Lok Sabha approval. Even though the bill has not been passed, it shows the that the political branches of government have seriously considered implementing more gender diversity in public institutions. Although there are no gender or caste reservations in the Supreme Court or high courts, lower courts in India do have these reservations.

Do the Collegium's Judicial Appointments Reflect India's Prioritization of Gender and Caste Diversity?

To investigate whether the collegium's judicial appointments reflect the multiple layers of diversity in India, we conducted our own empirical analysis. We collected biographical characteristics of every judge appointed to the Supreme Court from its creation in 1950 until March 2018. We examined characteristics such as age at appointment, number of years as member of the bar, gender, caste and job that was held prior to their appointment. We compared the judges appointed by the executive-led system to the judges appointed by the collegium.[46] We used statistical tools that allowed us to determine whether any observed changes were due to random chance. Our research reveals a number of interesting trends.

First, our data show that both the total number of executive-led system and the total number of collegium-appointed judges are largely in proportion to the religious diversity of India. In terms of religious diversity, 79 per cent of executive-appointed judges were Hindu and 84 per cent of collegium-appointed judges were Hindu. According to the last census, approximately 80 per cent of Indians are Hindu.[47] Thus, judges of the Supreme Court since its inception have been fairly and proportionaly representative of the religious diversity of India.[48]

Second, judicial appointments by the collegium under the executive-led system roughly correspond to the regional diversity of India. There are twenty-nine states and seven union territories in India. There is a high court in most states, but some high courts have jurisdiction over more than one state. In total, there are twenty-five high courts. When comparing judges appointed by the executive to judges appointed by the collegium, we find that they appoint judges from each high court at roughly the same rates.[49] Thus, the collegium continues the executive-led system's policy of ensuring that the Court proportionally represents India's religious and regional diversity.[50]

Third, there has been very little caste diversity, under both the executive-led system or the collegium system. Nearly 25 per cent of India's population belongs to a scheduled caste or a scheduled tribe.[51]

However, as of 2018, only four per cent of all judges appointed by the executive (three judges) and less than one per cent of judges appointed by the collegium were from scheduled castes or scheduled tribes (one judge).[52] More recently, though the collegium has appointed two members of a scheduled caste (Justice C.T. Ravikumar in 2021 and Justice Bhushan R. Gavai in 2019), the point still remains that the appointments have not been representative of the Indian population. Given that over time one might expect that the representation of scheduled castes and scheduled tribes would rise, this lack of positive change—and in fact, change in the opposite direction—suggests that the collegium system has not been accompanied by an emphasis on the elevation of judges from scheduled castes to the higher echelons of the judiciary.

Fourth, the collegium's appointment of female judges is similarly problematic. Only seven out of 116 judges appointed to the Court by the collegium as of May 2019 have been women, and only three new female judges (Justices Hima Kohli, B.V. Nagarathna and Bela Trivedi) have been appointed since 2019. To date, only eleven of the 266 judges who have served (or are currently serving) on the Supreme Court have been women. Only about 4 per cent of all judges sitting on the Court have been female. There is no statistically significant difference in the share of judges who are female among the executive-appointed and collegium-appointed judges, although the difference is a large increase in percentage terms (1 per cent pre-collegium versus 5 per cent under the collegium, corresponding to one and seven women justices [as of 2018] respectively).

Although this small increase is better than no increase, one might ask whether the collegium ushered in an immediate increase in the rate at which women justices were appointed, or whether the increase over time simply reflected a gradual trend, perhaps due to increasing numbers of women in the legal profession. To answer this question, we used a statistical tool called regression analysis to see if the collegium had any effect on gender diversity that was different from just the continuation of a gradual trend of increasing representation of women on the Court. What we found was that the collegium is associated with no increase in the share of women justices over time. In other words, while there is a gradual trend over time of more women justices, the creation of the collegium does not mark any increase in the share of women justices at that time.

An analysis of the appointment of high court justices also reveals the lack of attention to gender diversity on the part of the collegium. The collegium draws heavily upon judges from the pool of high court chief justices. As of 2018, 86 per cent of collegium-appointed judges were high court chief justices (whereas only 53 per cent of the executive-appointed judges were Chief Justices of a high court). If the collegium desired to increase the gender diversity of the Court, the collegium would prioritize appointment of female high court chief justices to the Supreme Court

However, we found that the collegium does not appear to prefer appointments of female chief justices of high courts to the Supreme Court. Among male chief justices in our sample, about 36 per cent were elevated to the Court, while only 25 per cent of female chief justices in the sample were elevated to the Court. Although not statistically significant, this difference is troubling.

Only twelve out of 242 judges in our high court chief justice dataset are women—that is less than 5 per cent of the total. Thus, even if *every single* woman who is chief justice of a high court in our data were elevated to the Court, women would comprise barely 10 per cent of the total number of Supreme Court judges (there have been twelve women high court chief justices and 116 Supreme Court judges in the collegium period in our data as of 2018). Moreover, what we observe is that women high court chief justices are being appointed at a low rate relative to men.

The lower rate of appointment of women high court chief justices to the Court cannot be easily attributed to women chief justices having less experience or seniority than the male counterparts. Among those chief justices elevated to the Court, tenure in the lower courts is nearly the same for men and women (14.0 years and 14.7 years, respectively). Male and female chief justices are appointed at basically the same age (58.9 years for men and 59.6 years for women). Among those who were later elevated to the Court, the age at appointment as chief justice is slightly higher for women (59.3 versus 57.9 for men), but again the difference is not statistically significant. Male and female chief justices have nearly the same experience as members of the bar pre-appointment (22.8 years for men and 21.8 years for women).

There is an indication, if anything, that women chief justices have to be *more* qualified than men to be appointed to the Court. Women chief justices are statistically significantly more likely than men to have been appointed chief justice in another high court (19 per cent of male chief justices and 50 per cent of female chief justices, statistically significant at the 1-percent level). In other words, women chief justices, on average, have experience across more high courts during their careers as chief justices.[53] A feminist critique would posit that this means that women have to work harder than men to get the same jobs.

Given these patterns in the data, we see clear implications for how the Court could, if it wished to, increase its gender diversity. If the collegium is committed to drawing judges primarily from the pool of high court chief justices, it should appoint women to the position of high court chief justices at a very high rate to make a dent in the lack of gender diversity on the Supreme Court. Given that there is also a seniority norm that governs who becomes a chief justice of a high court, women must also be appointed to high courts at younger ages than they are now and/or that the seniority norm for high court chief justice appointments not be followed in some cases.

Not only does the Supreme Court not reflect India's gender and caste diversity but neither do the high courts. A 2011 report of the National Commission for scheduled castes reported that there were only twenty-one judges from scheduled castes and scheduled tribes in high courts and fourteen out of twenty-four high courts did not have a single judge from these communities.[54] Some have suggested that as of 2016, only eighteen of the 600 judges in high courts were from under-represented castes.[55] As of 2019, there are sixty-nine women judges in high courts around the country, which is less than 11 per cent of the total.

Appointments of judges (other than the chief justice) of high courts are initiated by a collegium of justices of the high court. This collegium proposes names to the Supreme Court collegium, which ultimately decides which of those nominees are appointed or rejected. One author posits that high court collegiums are not putting forward a proportional number of women to men.[56] The study finds that between October 2017 and April 2019, of the total number of candidates considered for high court judgeship, 88 per cent were men while 12 per cent were women.[57] The study further shows that of the people nominated by the high court collegiums, the Supreme Court collegium accepts roughly the same proportion of women and men. In other words, even though the high courts are nominating far fewer women than men, the Supreme Court does not disproportionately appoint the female nominees.[58]

Some might argue that there is a pipeline problem, i.e., there just are not enough women lawyers who could be appointed to the judiciary. This would have been the case for appointments made under the pre-1993 system, but that situation has changed during the collegium period. While we were not able to find national data straddling the pre-collegium and collegium periods, we do have regional data that suggests that the ratio of women lawyers relative to male lawyers increased dramatically from the pre-collegium to the collegium period. In the state of Uttar Pradesh, during the period between 1962 and 1997, 3.12 per cent of all lawyers that registered were women. But from 1998 to 2005, 12.3 per cent of the lawyers that registered were women.[59] In Delhi, we observe a similarly large increase in the number of female practising lawyers. From 1981 to 1990, women were only 8.1 per cent of lawyers, but from 1991 to 2000, women constituted 22 per cent of all lawyers.[60]

The government recently released data (though it was far from complete) that showed that overall 15 per cent of lawyers are women. Assuming this data is accurate and has been constant for some period of time, the Supreme Court today should consist of 15 per cent of women or somewhere near that number.[61] At the time this book goes to press, there are three women out of thirty-four judges, which is approximately 9 per cent. Thus, the gender composition of the Court is closer to representing the percentage of female lawyers than it is to representing the number of women in the population, but it still falls short.

On the other hand, while the higher judiciary is not proportionally representative of caste and gender, the lower judiciary, which is under the control of state governments, is more diverse. Some of those governments have implemented quotas for women and underrepresented groups. In Delhi, 20 per cent of judicial posts are reserved for scheduled castes and 12 per cent for scheduled tribes. Tamil Nadu and Andhra Pradesh have reserved seats for women.[62] Over time, the collegium has failed to keep up with the changing political landscape in India that favours more proportional representation for women and disadvantaged classes of society.

Conclusion

It appears that the collegium has a notion of diversity that focuses on only regional and religious diversity. However, the collegium has not kept pace with new notions of diversity supported by the political branches, namely gender and caste diversity.

The collegium's lack of appointments to reflect the proportional representation of women and caste minorities is particularly problematic in light of the changing political landscape. There has been an increasing use of quotas for women and underrepresented caste minorities in public institutions as a way to promote equality. While there is no doubt that the issue of reservations is a contentious one, with many opponents of reservation in public educational institutions and otherwise, policies and legislative changes have still moved towards ensuring that women and scheduled castes and scheduled tribes are represented appropriately in public institutions. Indeed, the Parliament required that at least one member of the proposed commission be a woman or scheduled caste or scheduled tribe member.

Some might be concerned that diversity will come at the cost of quality. There is no evidence for this, however. To the contrary, there is every reason not to be concerned. There are only thirty-four seats on the Supreme Court, in a country of more than one billion people. There are many skilled high court judges (of different castes and genders) throughout India—more than enough to ensure that the

Supreme Court could be filled with a judges who are both excellent and diverse.

The only way to change the appointment procedure of the Court would be for the Parliament to pass another amendment to the Constitution and the Court to declare it constitutional. The *Fourth Judges Case* did not suggest that no mechanism other than the collegium would satisfy the Court. It found that the structure adopted by the Parliament at that time was not acceptable, but a different mechanism could be. Perhaps a commission where judges had primacy in decisions would pass scrutiny under the basic structure doctrine.

As long as the collegium system is in place, the collegium should consider altering the appointments process to make the Court reflect a broader notion of diversity. The collegium members could appoint more women and caste minorities to high courts with an eye to ensuring that they will eventually be senior enough to be chief justices of high courts and therefore, be stronger candidates for appointment to the Supreme Court.

Vice Chancellor Raj Kumar has proposed a bolder solution—that the collegium should be amended so that it always includes one woman and presumably also one scheduled caste or scheduled tribe member.[63] Although there is no guarantee that by simply adding one woman or scheduled caste or tribe member in the collegium will increase the number of female or minority judges that are eventually nominated by the collegium, empircal studies conducted on U.S. federal appeals courts suggest that when female judges are on panels with male judges, they do influence the decisions of their male colleagues in some cases.[64] Reforms such as these would be one step toward a more diverse Supreme Court. The collegium, however, may not have enough internal incentive to achieve more gender and caste diversity on the Court.

6

Pandering to the Political Branches: Short Tenures and Early Retirements

Just four months after he retired as the Chief Justice of India, Justice Ranjan Gogoi shook up the legal establishment by accepting a nomination to the Rajya Sabha offered by the President. Although most members of the upper house of Parliament are elected by state legislatures, the executive has the ability to nominate a few people. Numerous leading scholars and lawyers have argued that Justice Gogoi's appointment undermines judicial independence.[1] For example, Pratap Bhanu Mehta argued that Justice Gogoi's actions will 'cast doubt on the Court as a whole; every judgment will now be attributed to political motives'.[2]

The uproar against Gogoi might seem to imply that it is unusual for a retired Supreme Court judge to be given a prestigious government post after retiring, but that is not true. Most retired Supreme Court judges seek employment upon retirement from the Court and the single biggest employer of retired judges is the government.

Supreme Court judges take up post-retirement posts because they must retire at sixty-five from the Court.[3] The sixty-five-year age limit is a holdover from the era of colonial courts. Today it seems relatively young given that life expectancy has increased.

The concern with an early retirement age is that it incentivizes judges to pander to the party from whom they are seeking jobs. The government is the biggest litigator before the Court and it has also been the largest employer of retired judges. The fear that judges will pander to the government in their decisions has been demonstrated by a recent empirical study.[4] Another challenge of the early retirement age combined with the fact that the judges that are appointed to be chief justices are the senior most judges in the court, is that recent chief justices have been in the position for an average of nine months. Given the outsized role the Chief Justice plays in the administering the judicial system, this revolving door creates significant instability for the Court. In addition, judges spend on average five years on the Court, which may also lead to doctrinal instability.

The Retirement Age Dates Back to British Colonial Courts

The Constitution of India states that judges of the Supreme Court must retire when they reach the age of sixty-five.[5] The retirement age of the Federal Court of India was sixty-five years, and the retirement age of the colonial high courts was sixty. Unable to agree on a higher or lower retirement age, the framers of the Indian Constitution adopted the age set for colonial courts. [6] In 1963, the Constitution was amended to increase the retirement age of high court judges from sixty to sixty-two. However, no changes have been made to the retirement age of the judges of the Supreme Court.

Some members of the Constituent Assembly proposed that the retirement age for judges of the Indian Supreme Court should be higher than for the colonial apex court. Shibban Lal Saksena looked to England and America and pointed out that judges in the United States and United Kingdom have no retirement age, but rather life tenure. He believed that life tenure 'contributes to their independence in giving judgments'.[7] B. Pocker Sahib Bahadur added that a retirement age of sixty-five means that some judges 'who are very energetic and who are well fitted to discharge the duties for a number of years more' retire.[8] Other members supported raising the retirement age on the basis of a report submitted by the judges of the Federal Court and high courts supporting a retirement age of sixty-eight for the Supreme Court and sixty-five for the high courts.[9]

A second group of arguments favoured adopting a lower retirement age for judges of the Indian Supreme Court than the prior colonial apex court. Jaspat Roy Kapoor suggested three reasons to lower the age of retirement. Firstly, he noted that the age of retirement of government civil servants is fifty-five and of high court judges is sixty, so he saw no reason to extend the age of retirement of Supreme Court judges to sixty-five. He thought '[t]hey must, after putting in long years of service, retire and make room for others to come in.'[10]

Secondly, he proposed that 'very often a person who has gone beyond the age of sixty is not very fit and is not mentally alert to perform the strenuous duties of a judge of the Supreme Court'[11] so he believed that a retirement age of sixty-five would be unsafe.[12] K.M. Munshi also agreed that 'at the age of sixty most of the judges of the high court—I do not say all—become unfit for further continuance on the bench.'[13] Another member, T.T. Krishnamachari, noted that in 'about 30 per cent of the cases perhaps, people who attain the age of sixty become unfit for active work.'[14] Lastly, he proposed that judges should be prepared to serve society in an honorary capacity from the age of sixty.[15]

A final proposal was to let the Parliament fix the retirement age instead of crystallizing it in the Constitution. Satish Chandra noted that '[t]he question of age is one which can be left safely to the future parliaments to be decided and fixed, in particular circumstances, according to the needs and exigencies of the time.'[16]

There were some members who were satisfied with the retirement age of sixty-five. M. Ananthasayanam Ayyangar, for example, said that the age of sixty-five is young enough to ensure that those on the court are still of a 'balanced mind' but high enough to ensure that justices have 'sufficient experience' to 'judge calmly and coolly'.[17]

Foreshadowing the problems we see today, other Constituent Assembly members proposed that a fixed retirement age be abolished, in the interests of judicial independence. Member K.T. Shah suggested that the Constitution provide for life appointments since the lure of post-retirement government appointments could influence a judge's decisions while on the bench. He noted that judges facing post-retirement government appointments were at risk of making decisions which 'may not be in tune with their perfect independence and integrity'.[18]

There was a difference in the retirement age for judges on the Federal Court of India and the colonial high courts—with judges of the high court being required to retire at sixty. The rationale for the gap in the retirement ages of the apex court as compared to the high court was to encourage high court judges to take posts in the Federal Court.[19] At the time the Federal Court of India was created, high courts were already in place and so it was thought that some judges might feel it was more prestigious to remain in the high court rather than take a post in the Federal Court of India. By setting the retirement age at sixty of the high courts, it meant that the retiring judges of the high courts were more likely to seek a position in the Federal Court of India. Eventually, the constitutional framers retained the same retirement ages for the post-independence courts as the ones that existed for the colonial era courts.

The current retirement ages in the high courts and Supreme Court reflect a colonial-era rationale, and this rationale no longer applies today, as Abhinav Chandrachud has argued.[20] Unlike jobs on the Federal Court of India, postings to the Supreme Court are prestigious and high court judges are likely to take them even if the retirement ages in the high courts were the same as in the Supreme Court. Nonetheless, this gap remains. In 1963, the Parliament amended the Constitution to increase the retirement age of high court judges to sixty-two years,[21] but proposals to increase the retirement age of high courts even further to sixty-five have failed.[22]

Judges Need Employment After They Retire

Life expectancy at birth in India was 41.4 years in 1960 and in 2017, it was 69.2 years.[23] When the Federal Court of India was conceived in

1937, the life expectancy was even lower—it was around thirty years.[24] Life expectancy has increased over the decades, particularly for the wealthy. Indeed, recent data shows that life expectancy at birth is 65.1 years for the poorest fifth of households in India and 72.7 years for the richest fifth of households.[25] People who become judges of the Indian Supreme Court today are from the wealthier sections of society and their life expectancy is likely closer to the richest households in India. Evidence of the increasing life expectancy of Indian Supreme Court judges is that up through 2000, twelve judges died in office.[26] On the other hand, since 2000, only one judge on the Indian Supreme Court has died in office.[27]

With life expectancy increasing, judges now have a greater life span post-retirement than they previously did. There are many reasons judges would want to work after retirement, one of which is that they need to supplement their pension to maintain the lifestyle they had when they were sitting judges. Sitting Supreme Court judges are allowed to reside in sprawling estates in central Delhi. After retirement, however, a Supreme Court judge is not granted a residence and their pension does not match their pre-retirement salary.[28] Yet, the Constitution prohibits retired judges from doing one of the most lucrative things they could do—return to private practice.[29]

As a result, historically, a significant number of judges obtain employment from the government. Today there are more even government jobs available for retired judges with the growth of specialized tribunals and commissions, some of which require that the members be former justices of the Supreme Court. It should be noted that over the last decade or so a new form of employment has also become available to judges. With the increase of out-of-court private arbitration, retired Supreme Court judges are often hired to sit as arbitrators.

The Government: A Major Litigator Before the Supreme Court

During the Constituent Assembly debates, K. T. Shah warned that the high court and Supreme Court judges should not take up a job from the government, 'so that no temptation should be available to a judge for greater emoluments, or greater prestige which would in any way affect his independence as a judge'.[30] However, B.R. Ambedkar rejected this proposal because he thought the judiciary would not decide many cases where the government has a great interest. Thus, he noted that 'the chances of influencing the conduct of a member of the judiciary by the government are very remote'.[31]

Ambedkar's prediction, however, turned out to be inaccurate. The government appears before the Supreme Court in a significant number of cases. Others have noted that the government is the most frequent party in litigation before the Court.[32] Our review of all published cases by the Supreme Court from 2010 to 2014, supports this conclusion. We found that government is the appellant in roughly 20 per cent of the cases. It is the respondent in 54 per cent percent of cases. (These categories overlap, because in about 1 per cent of the cases, the government is on both sides.) Thus, in total, the government is a party in approximately 73 per cent of the cases in our data of Supreme Court cases though not all of these cases are high profile ones.

Judges Pander to the Government

An influential study by the Bingham Centre for the Rule of Law at the British Institute of International and Comparative Law (the 'Bingham Centre Report') recognizes the problems of early retirement ages and government jobs. The report notes that 'problems are likely to arise in situations where the retirement age is low and judges may be eligible for lucrative or prestigious post-retirement positions over which the government has a significant influence . . .'[33] The Bingham Centre report rightly recognizes the problems for judicial independence when the retirement age is set too low and government is one of the largest post-retirement employers.

What is more troubling is that a new empirical study suggests that Indian Supreme Court judges do in fact pander to the government when they are likely to be able to obtain government jobs. In their paper, *Jobs for Justice(s): Corruption in the Supreme Court of India*,

Madhav Aney, Shubhankar Dam and Giovanni Ko[34] constructed a dataset of cases decided by the Supreme Court of India between 1999 and 2014 involving the government. They analysed the full text of the judgments and coded whether the government won or lost the case. In total, they examined 652 cases, which were 25 per cent of the 2605 reported cases involving the Union of India from 1999 to 2014.

The goal of this study was to look for evidence that judges decided cases in favour of the government as they approached retirement. The theory is that because the government is the biggest employer of retired judges, judges need to appease the government so that they have better employment opportunities after mandatory retirement from the Court. To be clear, this study was not about explicit corruption, such as bribes. Rather, it was about the influence (even subconsciously) of employment incentives in judicial decisions that are supposed to be based on the facts and the law, not pandering to the preferences of a powerful litigant.

The influence of employment incentives is not easy to detect. Judges who are influenced would not admit it, and if the influence is subconscious, they may not even realize it themselves. Further, not every judge and not every case will be affected by this influence. So what Aney, Dam and Ko did was look for patterns in the data that would reveal this hidden influence. Their strategy was to compare cases where the incentive to pander to the government was greatest with cases where the incentive was weaker, and then see if judges behaved differently when they had different incentives.

The strongest incentive for a judge to pander would be in deciding a case in which the government is a litigant, the judge is close to retirement and there is no election coming soon. Because there is no election coming soon, the judge will know that the same government that is litigating the case will still be in power when the judge seeks a job after retirement. In this situation, the judge will have a strong incentive to decide in favour of the government. In contrast, the incentive is weaker if the judge is close to retirement, but there is an election coming soon. Because an election is looming, the control of the government may change, and the judge does not know whether the same government will be in place at the time they retire.

They compared the behaviour of judges who retired close to an election against the behaviour of judges who retired when an election was farther away (i.e., sixteen months after their retirement date). They theorized that judges are more likely to issue pro-government decisions when there is not likely to be immediate government turnover after their retirement. In other words, they believed, and their data proves, that judges are more likely to issue pro-government decisions when there is less risk that the government might turnover in an election for a period of time after their retirement. Alternatively, Supreme Court judges are less likely to rule in favour of the government when their retirement is closer to an election. The authors assume that judges are uncertain about who the new government will be after an election and therefore, lack incentive to rule in favour of the existing government. Thus, the authors further found that judges are more likely to issue pro-government decisions if they retire father away from an election than those who retire close to an election.

Most remarkably, they found that judges who authored favourable judgments in important cases were more likely to receive prestigious government jobs. Thus, not only do judges need jobs after retirement, but this data indicates that judges are pandering to the government in their decisions and are in fact being rewarded for it through jobs. This suggests that the early retirement age has created perverse incentives for how cases are decided. Judges should only weigh the merits of the cases of both parties rather than be motivated by other incentives such as post-retirement jobs.

The Revolving Door of Chief Justices of India

Another set of problems that arise because of the early retirement age is that chief justices spend a short amount of time in their positions. Chief Justices are required to retire at sixty-five just like other judges on the Supreme Court, but a judge can only be appointed a chief justice if she is the senior-most judge on the Court.

As early as 1958, the Law Commission of India recognized that in order to 'render that necessary and useful service which is expected of the Chief Justice', he should have a tenure of at least five to seven years.[35] They also recognized that the seniority norm created a situation where judges only held the position of Chief Justice of India (CJI) for a short period of time. As such, the Commission advocated moving away from the principle of seniority and having an alternative method of appointment.[36]

But just twenty years later, the commission backed away from this position after the country saw the executive's efforts to pack the Court by appointing judges that were pro-government to the post of CJI (as discussed in Chapter 5).[37] Thus, the rule that only the senior-most judges are appointed to the post of CJI remains in place today.

The average tenure of CJIs from when the Court was founded in 1950 until 2018 was eighteen months. Of the ten justices to retire from April 2014 to August 2022, their average tenure as CJI was 264 days, which is about nine months. The longest serving CJI was Y. V. Chandrachud who was CJI for 7.3 years and the shortest serving CJI was Kamal Narain Singh who served for less than three weeks.

Bert Neuborne notes the practice of appointing the senior-most judge as CJI 'results in a revolving-door Chief Justiceship'.[38] Indeed, there have been fifty-four chief justices from 1950 to 2018. As a result of this high turnover, Neuborne argues that it is 'virtually impossible for a chief justice to initiate significant changes . . . or to make a substantive mark on the law'.[39]

The CJI is the Master of the Roster and that gives him a lot of unchecked discretion as we discussed in Chapter 4. There are downsides with constantly changing who has this power. When the person wielding this unchecked and unregulated power keeps changing, it will no doubt lead to institutional instability. What one CJI thinks is an institutional priority to address some of the systemic concerns with the Court, another CJI might disagree with. Thus, these institutional priorities might change rapidly given that no one CJI stays in power for very long.

Indian Supreme Court Judges Spend Less than Five Years on the Bench on Average

An early commentator of the Court, American political scientist George Gadbois, observed in 1969 that the average tenure of Supreme Court judges was 6.6 years.[40] Over time, this number has gone down as judges join the Court at older ages, but still must retire at age sixty-five. Supreme Court judges who were appointed on or after April 2010 and who retired on or before April 2021, spent, on average, less than five years in office.[41]

As early as 1958, the Law Commission of India also observed the need for judges of the Indian Supreme Court to have longer tenures. The Commission noted that '[i]n our view, it is undesirable that a person who would have a short tenure of office . . . be chosen as a Judge of the Court. It is imperative in the interests of the stability of the judicial administration of the country that a Judge of the Supreme Court . . . have a tenure of office of at least ten years.'[42] When judges spend such a short period of time on the Supreme Court, there can be problematic results, including varying adherence to precedent as judicial philosophies are changing with the revolving door of judges.[43]

Judges in Apex Courts Around the World Spend More Time on the Bench

Courts around the world typically fall into one of three categories. First, in some countries, apex court judges are appointed for life. In those courts, judges leave the court when they resign or die in office. Second, other countries impose term limits for apex court judges. This means that judges must retire after a set number of years. Finally, like India, some courts have a fixed retirement age for judges.

Only a minority of courts provide life tenure for judges. According to the CIA Factbook, less than 15 per cent of courts around the world guarantee life tenure to their judges. The United States Supreme Court is one such court. Approximately 40 per cent of all apex courts have term limits. Interestingly, in 70 per cent of courts with term limits, the term limit for judges is greater than six years. As discussed above, the modern data suggests that on average a judge serves less than five years on the Court. Thus, even if the judges of the Indian Supreme Court had term limits of six years, they would still spend more time on the bench than they currently do.

About 45 per cent of the courts in the world have a retirement age. The majority (61 per cent) of the countries that have retirement ages have set their ages higher than the Indian Supreme Court's retirement age. For example, the retirement age of judges of the Canadian Supreme Court is seventy-five,[44] whereas the retirement age for judges of the UK Supreme Court and the Japanese Supreme Court is seventy.[45] Consequently, with a mandatory retirement age of sixty-five and an average time on the bench of less than five years, the judges of the Indian Supreme Court spend less time on the Court than a significant number of judges on apex courts around the world.

This pattern remains true even if we focus only on courts in commonwealth countries. There is no commonwealth jurisdiction where judges are appointed for life.[46] South Africa is the only country that has adopted a fixed term appointment for judges. Judges of the constitutional court must retire after twelve to fifteen years depending on whether the appointee previously held judicial office.[47] Most courts of commonwealth countries, however, do have mandatory retirement ages.

83 per cent of commonwealth countries that have retirement ages for judges have set the age higher than set for Indian Supreme Court judges. None have a lower retirement age. Of the forty-three commonwealth countries (excluding India),[48] the retirement ages of the highest courts are as follows:

- Twenty-nine countries have a retirement age of seventy or above: this includes those countries where a retirement age was less than 70 but could be extended to seventy or above (67 per cent)
- Seven countries have a retirement age of sixty-eight (16 per cent)
- Seven countries have a retirement age of sixty-five (16 per cent)[49]
- No country has a retirement age lower than sixty-five[50]

Increasing the Retirement Age

We suggest that the Parliament should amend the Constitution to increase the retirement age of the judges of the Indian Supreme Court to seventy years of age. Even if the Parliament does not act to increase the retirement age, we recommend that the collegium ensure that when they nominate judges, they have a term of at least seven years. In other words, they would have to appoint people at a younger age than they currently do.

In a recent report, the Law Commission of India also suggested that the retirement age be increased by 'at least three years'.[51] It later noted that the question of increasing the retirement age for Supreme Court judges to seventy has 'been a matter of serious discussion/ consideration'[52] and that 'retirement age in many government departments/disciplines . . . has already been increased'.[53] A retirement age of seventy would also bring the Indian Supreme Court in line with courts around the world. An influential report of courts of commonwealth countries, the Bingham report, concludes that the 'best practice in modern conditions would probably require the mandatory age be set at, or closer to, 70 years'.[54] In addition, we recommend that judges receive the same benefits and salary after retirement that they received while they were sitting judges. These benefits will reduce the pressure on judges to pander to the government in order to secure jobs after mandatory retirement from the Court.

There will be several benefits to our proposals. First, judges will be less likely to need to take post-retirement jobs since the time they are less likely to need to work past seventy years of age as compared to sixty. This would avoid any actual and potential conflicts when they hear cases by or against the government given that retired currently judges often take jobs offered by the government. If judges have the same salary and benefit after retirement, it would reduce their incentives to take post-retirement jobs.

Second, the tenures of judges will increase (assuming that the age of appointment does not increase). This will ensure more precedential and administrative continuity. Third, raising the retirement age of

Supreme Court judges could reduce the seniority imbalance between senior advocates and judges and thereby decrease the power of senior advocates (as discussed in greater detail in Chapter 3).

Other proposals for reform have also been made to address the problems discussed in this chapter. Some authors have suggested that judges should be prohibited from taking employment from the government after retirement as a way to avoid perception of lack of independence.[55] During the Constituent Assembly debates, one member, Mr. Santhanam, also proposed that '[j]udicial officers, especially of the highest rank should never be induced to accept any government job. When they retire, they should never look up to government for some sort of job after their judicial career is ended.'[56] The problem with this is that without post-retirement employment from the government, some judges may not be able to find jobs at all. Although arbitration for commercial disputes is increasing in India and former Supreme Court judges are increasingly serving as arbitrators, many former judges still take up government-offered jobs after retirement.

Others have suggested a less drastic measure—a cooling off period before a judge accepts a government job.[57] Sengupta, for example, suggests a cooling off period of three years assuming retirement age stays sixty-five.[58] The problem with this is that it creates a situation where judges are not employed for a significant amount of time after retirement. This could face resistance among judges because after retirement, judges do not have the same salary and benefits that they did before retirement. However, this problem could be addressed by ensuring that retiring judges have the same benefits and pension after they retire as they did when they were sitting judges.

On the other hand, we recognize that increasing the retirement age of Supreme Court judges could also have problematic unintended consequences. For example, certain specialized tribunals mandate that former Supreme Court judges be appointed to them. Assuming that at the point that they reach seventy, returning judges no longer wish to work, the government will to open up those jobs to non-Supreme Court judges.

Some people have objected to raising the retirement age. A relatively young retirement age and a short tenure of judges allows new perspectives to enter the bench. A Rajya Sabha committee evaluating whether to increase the retirement age of high court judges suggested that judges should retire to make room for new blood.[59] The problem with this argument is that it ignores the empirical reality that there is already a lot of turnover on the Court, which has thirty-four judge positions. But this turnover comes with great costs. Increasing the retirement age would still mean there is a turnover and fresh perspectives entering the Court, but no so much turnover that the challenges of administration persist.

We do not recommend giving life tenure to judges, however. Increasing the retirement age rather than granting life tenure ensures that there is still enough turnover to include fresh and diverse perspectives on the Court. Another option for the Parliament is to adopt term limits, but the problem is that it does not remove incentives to pander to future employers. The risk is that judges could be appointed at young ages and when they reach their term limit, they retire when they also have a long life ahead of them.

In sum, chief justices and judges have very short tenures on the Court. While chief justices have tenures of only about nine months, the average tenure of all judges on the Supreme Court is little more than five years. This compromises institutional and precedential stability. The tenures of judges are even shorter than courts that have fixed terms for judges. A significant majority of commonwealth countries have a retirement age of seventy or more for judges on apex courts. Increasing the retirement age would require a constitutional amendment, but there are a number of benefits in doing so. If the retirement age were raised, judges would likely have longer tenures thereby increasing institutional stability and judges will also have less incentive to pander to the government as they are less likely to need post-retirement jobs. Finally, we note that to avoid appearing as though it is favouring existing judges, if the government does amend the Constitution to increase the retirement age, the new policy should apply only to new judges that join the Court.

7

Conclusion: An Accountable Court

As India emerged from British colonial rule, the drafters of the Indian Constitution enshrined in it a robust set of individual rights and put in place a range of norms and institutions to promote the rule of law and make democracy work. They reposed a lot of trust in the Indian judiciary, and particularly the Supreme Court, in securing these rights, enforcing these norms, holding the State to account, and fostering the rule of law. The Supreme Court's own vision for its role in India's constitutional democracy also mirrors these aspirations. However, in the almost seventy-five years of its existence, its own institutional structure and processes have started working at cross-purposes with its best impulses.

The India of today, as well the Court of today, looks very different from the Court in 1950. What started as a small court of eight judges, sitting in large benches, hearing a small number of matters, and focusing its energies on expounding the new Constitution, has now become a behemoth of 34 judges, struggling to keep up with the demand for its time, sitting in smaller and smaller benches, hearing more and more matters, and so swamped with routine appeals that it does not have the time to devote to the most pressing issues of the day. This shift has been organic, the product of the Court's changing conception of its role in the Indian polity—a shift that has been geared towards greater access to the Court for combating rights violations and governmental lawlessness.[1] However, though the shift in the Court's role has been intentional,[2] very little reflection has gone into how the institutional design and processes of the Court should keep up with the changing role of the Court.

In this book, we have evaluated the functioning of the Supreme Court using hard data on the decisions of the Court, the lawyers who appear before the Court, the cases brought to the Court, the judges of the Court and other information. We have used sophisticated empirical research tools that allow us to see trends and patterns in the data. Our data does not single out the behaviour or attributes of any one judge, lawyer or other actor, but rather reveals aggregate information. Using these methods, we have exposed new information about the Supreme Court, including the powerful influence of senior advocates to the fact that the problem of delay is as great in the Supreme Court as it is in the lower courts. Many of the problems that we highlight in this book are already topics of conversation within legal circles. But by using hard data to understand the nature, scope and extent of these problems as well as possible solutions, our aim has been to move the conversation about the Court beyond opinion, conjecture and anecdotes, to evidence-based reform. For far too long, conversation on the Court and its reform have been based on impressionistic, anecdotal tales often derived from a few high-profile cases, rather than on overall trends and patterns based on rigorous studies. For a public institution that wields such immense public power, the lack of robust data on the Court also shields it from public scrutiny by shrouding the Court and its functioning in opacity, mystification, and a constructed image of working for the public good.

However, as this book reveals, many of the claims that the Court makes for itself, do not stand up to scrutiny. The institutional processes and administrative structures of the Court are often working at cross purposes with its constitutional role. These slippages between aim and approach are not by design, but through a lack of attention to the appropriate processes and structures that will enhance the functioning of the Court as it stands today. This limits the ability of the Court to live up to its promises and potentials. So, for example, though the Court claims to be a 'people's court' oriented towards access to justice, we find that its practices relating to admitting appeals limits the Court's ability to improve access to justice for the most marginalized. While the Court claims to decide cases on the basis of the rule of law, we find that the system of allocating cases to judges influences outcomes in the most important cases, and such allocation is not based on any rational principle. We find that these opaque administrative practices of allocating cases, listing cases, and (de-)prioritizing cases for hearing play an outsized role in ultimate outcomes on the judicial side—a classic case of the tail wagging the dog. Our aim through this study has been to make the opaque transparent, and thereby to enable greater scrutiny of the Court.

In some of the chapters, our findings are based on our own extensive data-gathering and analysis, but in others we have relied on the empirical work done by other scholars and organizations. It is important to acknowledge that quantitative empirical studies, like all forms of research, are never entirely free from error or possible biases from their design and data-gathering. However, by bringing more information into the conversation, this book brings everyone closer to better understanding an institution of central importance to the Indian polity.

In addition to shedding light on the practices of the Supreme Court, we have also attempted to offer solutions to the problems with the Court's functioning. We recognize that these solutions may be imperfect, and that changes to improve one court process can lead to unintended consequences by impacting other processes. With that caveat, we believe it was important to contribute to the on-going efforts towards court reform by having our data speak to these issues.

We find overall that the Court eschews attempts towards accountability for its actions by refusing to set clear standards to which it can be held accountable: it has refused to provide clear standards for appointing judges to the Court, on what basis such judges will admit cases for hearing, when such cases will actually come up for hearing and how judges will be allocated to hear such cases. The lack of clear standards is compounded by an abundance of opacity since the Court refuses to provide reasons for many of its administrative decisions, like the appointment of judges or the listing and allocation of cases. Taken together, the lack of clear standards, and the lack of information on the basis of its decisions, makes it difficult to scrutinize the actions of the Court and hold it to account for the immense public power that it wields.

Our study has been geared towards looking behind the curtain of opacity to understand how the Court is actually functioning, and why. Ultimately our comprehensive examination of the Supreme Court was conducted with the spirit of ensuring it functions more transparently, efficiently and justly. Below, we summarize some of our key findings in each chapter and our proposals for reform.

Chapter 1: A People's Court?

The Supreme Court envisions itself to be a court where the common person can get redress. Our research indicates that the Supreme Court is still a 'people's court', at least in one sense of the term. Our analysis of the data on Supreme Court cases provides evidence that the Court does give preferential treatment to the less powerful parties in litigation— individuals rather than corporations and accused persons rather than government prosecutors. This preferential consideration takes the form of a greater willingness of the Court to entertain petitions (SLPs) brought by relatively disadvantaged parties, even when the petitions are weak and unlikely to prevail after a full hearing. In other words, the disadvantaged may not be more likely to win in the end, but they are more likely to receive a full hearing from the Supreme Court.

This approach to being a 'people's court' by accepting many petitions may be well-intentioned, but it has backfired—the Court's huge caseload causes long delays, which are costly for the very parties it seeks to protect. The Court can also affect more cases involving disadvantaged parties by announcing rules for other courts to follow, rather than by deciding cases one-by-one. Even if disadvantaged groups have less access to the Supreme Court, announcing clear rules will provide them with more access to the lower courts. The Court gives broad access, but this broad access is indiscriminate. Instead, by focusing on cases that allow the Court to give clear guidance to all the judges of India, the Court could improve justice for Indians throughout the judicial system, not just those lucky or privileged enough to reach the Supreme Court. Broad access to those who have the resources to appear before it is a choice the Court has made and a choice the Court can change if it is determined to do so.

Chapter 2: Explosion, Exclusion, Evasion: The Burden of Backlogs

Studies indicate that in 2011, 17 per cent of the cases on the Supreme Court's regular hearing docket had been pending for more than five years, up from 7 per cent in 2004.[3] Since then, the backlog has grown worse. Our study, based on scraping data of all cases from the Supreme Court of India website, finds that as of November 2018, a whopping 40 per cent of cases in the Supreme Court were pending for more than five years, and an *additional* 8 per cent cases were pending for more than ten years. Yet some cases are resolved relatively quickly. Of cases disposed after both parties have appeared before the Court, half of them are concluded within about one and a half years from filing. Overall, then, the Supreme Court appears to provide two track justice—superfast disposals for some cases, and long gestation periods for others.

Although the problem of delay is often attributed to the lower courts, our data show that the Supreme Court has similarly long delays as other courts. In our data, cases that make it all the way from the trial court to the Supreme Court take, on average, around thirteen years and six months from first entering the judicial system to disposal by the Supreme Court. The Supreme Court itself accounts for about one-third of this total, approximately on a par with the average amount of time taken at each tier of the judiciary.[4]

The problem of delay in the Indian judicial system is not a new one. The long time frame for resolving cases is due to many factors,

including the increase in litigation being filed in India, limited judicial
resources and the Court's acceptance of a broad number of appeals. The
solutions we propose to increase the speed of Supreme Court decision-
making go beyond simply appointing more judges or staff at the Court.
We believe that the Court should take fewer cases, particularly special
leave petitions. The Court should allow the lower courts to resolve all
cases except those that raise new legal issues or legal issues for which
the Court can announce a new, clearer legal rule to aid the lower courts
in deciding future cases. We also note that the resources of the Court
are significantly taken up by oral hearings that span days. Much of
the work can be done through time-saving briefs and motions, with
oral hearing subject to firm, predictable time limits. Finally, the
government is one of the biggest litigators before the Court, but we
find that its success rate before the Court in the appeals that it brings is
quite limited. Government entities could therefore be more judicious
in bringing cases.

Chapter 3: 'Face Value': The Power and Influence of Senior Advocates

Lawyers who practise before the Court are well aware that senior
advocates—the hand-picked stars of the Supreme Court bar—exercise
influence over which cases the Supreme Court chooses to hear. Even
though senior advocates presumably have great skill at legal research
and assessing the merits of cases, we don't find evidence that the Court
relies on senior advocates to find better legal rules or separate weak
cases from strong cases. Instead, our research suggests that the Court
gravitates toward cases brought by senior advocates as a way to sort
through the overwhelming number of special leave petitions being filed
with the Court.

There is a paradox here. As we showed in Chapter 1, the Court
has loose standards for granting SLPs because it wants to be a 'people's
court', a court that allows access to petitioners, no matter how humble.
Yet, senior advocates are the key players who get SLPs admitted to the
Supreme Court and are the most expensive lawyers in India—some of

them are the most expensive lawyers in the world. Only the rich and powerful can afford to pay Rs 15 lakh for a lawyer to appear at a two-minute hearing.

In other words, the Supreme Court's approach to SLPs seeks to favour the common person for access to the Court, but at the same time, the Court heavily favours SLPs argued by the most expensive lawyers in the country. The Court gives access with one hand and takes it away with the other. This is neither good for the Court nor good for parties seeking access to the Court.

We offer a vision for fixing the relationship between senior advocates and the Supreme Court. Court reforms should seek buy-in from senior advocates. The goal of reform is not to diminish their power, but to better leverage their legal skill and expertise rather than merely their 'face value'. To this end, the Court should announce clear grounds for admitting SLPs. As we argued in Chapters 1 and 2, these grounds should include admitting only petitions that raise new legal issues or propose clear legal rules that provide guidance for all the courts of India. Such rules will focus the arguments made by senior advocates on legal issues that benefit the entire court system.

We also propose raising the mandatory retirement age for judges of the Supreme Court. Part of why senior advocates wield so much influence is that many of them have far more experience in the Supreme Court than the judges themselves, because the judges have relatively short tenures on the Court, usually five to seven years. If Supreme Court judges have more time on the Court, they can rely more on their own experience, and less on the greater seniority of senior advocates. There are other benefits of raising the retirement age as discussed in Chapter 6.

Chapter 4: First Amongst Equals? Master of the Roster and Strategic Case Assignments

The Chief Justice has an untrammelled power to assign judges to Constitution Benches. If this power were being deployed in a completely random manner, as if by lottery, we would expect that every judge would have a roughly equal likelihood of being on a Constitution Bench. We would expect that the Chief Justice would be in majority or in dissent in split decisions consistent with the patterns and rates of dissent of other judges or with their own overall dissent rates. Our analysis of the data, however, reveals that the assignment to larger benches, especially to Constitution Benches, is not random. Chief Justices over-assign themselves to Constitution Benches, while others are either completely frozen out or disproportionately favoured for inclusion. Further, while other judges dissent at higher rates on Constitution Benches, the Chief Justice is never in the dissent on a Constitution Bench. This implies that such benches are constituted in a manner that the Chief Justice always carries the majority with him, a feat that no other judge can equal. How then can the exercise of this power be constrained to limit its arbitrary or strategic exercise?

The norms and mechanisms by which administrative law holds public power to account in a democracy can guide us in designing a more accountable case allocation system. One solution for addressing the problem of strategic assignments by the Chief Justice is to remove discretion from the Chief Justice and automate assignments through mechanisms such as computerized allocations. A version of this approach is already in place for regular assignments to two-judge benches, so the technology is already available. Another oft-advocated approach to curtail the Chief Justice's discretion is to constitute one or more 'permanent Constitution Benches', that hear all pending matters without the need for case-specific assignments. Both these approaches will significantly curtail the Chief Justice's discretionary Master of the Roster power. In short, effective solutions to the Chief Justice's unchecked power over Constitution Benches are simple and feasible. The Court simply needs to be willing to implement them.

Chapter 5: People Like Us: Diversity (or Lack Thereof) in Judicial Appointments

The Indian Supreme Court has one of the most unusual appointment systems in the world. The Chief Justice of India and four of the senior-most judges of the Court at any given time nominate other judges to the

Court. The executive and the Parliament have little role in the process of judicial appointments. One of the fundamental values of democracy is that the government represents the people and ensuring that the judiciary has some connection to democratic processes, and that judges themselves share the diverse backgrounds of the people of the country, furthers a number of important values. Judges bring their own personal experiences to the decision-making process, and having judges who come from different backgrounds can lead to better decisions. When judges appoint each other, without any participation from the outside, the result may be the selection of a group of people who all hold the same views and are reluctant to disagree with each other. Diversity of experiences, perspectives and viewpoints may be lost.

Unfortunately, our data confirms that these concerns are real. The Court lacks diversity in important respects, and its caste and gender diversity over the past five decades has barely improved. Despite big advances for women and people of disadvantaged castes in the lower courts, local governments and other aspects of government, the collegium has not taken adequate steps to ensure that the Supreme Court reflects India's gender and caste diversity.

The Court rejected the Parliament's efforts to create a commission consisting of a broad range of actors that would nominate judges in the *Fourth Judges Case*. That case rejected the specific commission proposed by the Parliament, but it did not rule out other potential mechanisms. Perhaps a commission where judges had more of a primacy in decisions would be found constitutional.

As long as the collegium system is in place, the Chief Justice of India should consider a more deliberate approach towards making the appointments process reflect a broader notion of diversity. Because the collegium draws so heavily from chief justices of high courts in making its appointments, the key is for the collegium to appoint many more women and people of different castes to the high courts. This would ensure that the pool of high court chief justices will become more and more diverse over time, which in turn will allow the collegium's appointments of judges to the Supreme Court to finally bring significant gender and caste diversity to the Court.

Chapter 6: Pandering to the Political Branches: Short Tenures and Early Retirements

The Constitution requires judges to retire at sixty-five years of age. Because they retire at such a young age, they have a significant career ahead of them even after retirement. However, by law they are not permitted to work in private practice. In their groundbreaking empirical study, 'Jobs for Justice(s): Corruption in the Supreme Court of India', Madhav Aney, Shubhankar Dam and Giovanni Ko,[5] found evidence that as Supreme Court judges approach retirement, they tend to favour the government more and more in their decisions. This does not mean every judge panders, or that every case is affected by pandering, but it does mean that judges face powerful incentives to appease the government while they are on the Court, because their post-retirement employment may depend on it.

Judges of the Court are also appointed at late ages. As they are forced to retire at sixty-five, judges on the Court often spend less than five years in their jobs. A judge who is the most senior (based on years on the Court) becomes Chief Justice when the current Chief Justice retires. This means that Chief Justices have very short tenures—less than two years, on average. These short tenures undermine institutional and doctrinal stability.

To solve both the problem of pandering to the government, and the problem of institutional instability, we suggest that the Parliament should amend the Constitution to increase the retirement age of the judges of the Supreme Court to seventy years of age. A retirement age of seventy would bring the Supreme Court in line with courts around the world. Further, and even if the Parliament does not act to increase the retirement age, we recommend that the collegium ensure that when they nominate judges, they have a term of at least seven years. In other words, they would have to appoint people at a younger age than they currently do. Finally, we recommend that judges receive the same benefits and salary after retirement that they received while they were sitting judges.

There will be several benefits from our proposals. First, judges will be less likely to need to take post-retirement jobs since the time they need to support themselves after retirement will decrease. This would avoid any actual and potential conflicts when they hear cases by or against the government, given that retired currently judges often take jobs offered by the government. If judges have the same salary and benefit after retirement, then they may not need to take post-retirement jobs at all.

Second, the tenures of judges will increase (assuming that the age of appointment does not increase). This will ensure more precedential and administrative continuity. Third, raising the retirement age of Supreme Court judges will reduce the seniority imbalance between senior advocates and judges and will decrease the power of senior advocates as further discussed in Chapter 3.

Conclusion

The Supreme Court of India sits atop the largest court system of any democracy in the world. Its judgments announce legal rules for, and can affect the lives of nearly one and half billion people. When the Court functions well, the benefits are immense. When it is hobbled by delay, inconsistency, bias or conflicts of interest, the potential costs are equally massive. Thus, when considering the possibilities for reforms to improve the work of the Court, the stakes are high, and reforms should be guided by extensive data and careful analysis, with an eye towards making the functioning of the Court more transparent, accountable, equitable, efficient and just. This book seeks to provide one attempt at such data and analysis, in service of the world's most important court.

Acknowledgements

The project that ultimately culminated into this book began over a decade ago. It was in part the brainchild of Theodore Eisenberg, professor of law at Cornell Law School, who pioneered empirical legal studies and used empirical tools to describe and analyse the US courts and courts globally. He passed away suddenly and far too soon in 2014. We continued the work we started with him and produced several pieces that finally culminated in this book.

The University of Chicago India Center, the Jerome F. Kutak Faculty Fund, the Coase-Sandor Institute for Law & Economics, and the Cornell Law School provided generous financial support for this project. We received important feedback from numerous workshops, including at Cornell Law School, University of Chicago Law School, Columbia Law School, University of Chicago India Center in New Delhi, Indian Law Institute, Empirical Legal Studies conferences, Law and Society Association, and Law and Social Science Research Network conferences. We also received helpful comments from many scholars, judges and lawyers—among them are Nick Robinson, Justice Madan Lokur, Justice S. Muralidhar, Professor Upendra Baxi, Rajeev Dhavan, late Soli Sorabjee, Mohan Gopal, Justice S. B. Sinha, Justice Ravindra Bhat, Justice Gita Mittal, Justice T. S. Thakur, Liz Mathew, Tarunabh Khaitan, Sudhir Krishnaswamy, Abhinav Chandrachud, C. Raj Kumar and Gerry Rosenberg. Our graduate students and research assistants including Krithika Ashok, Sakina Haji, Shubho Roy and Caroline Veniero provided valuable feedback and research on the manuscript.

Our institutional homes, Cornell Law School, National Law School of India University, Bengaluru, National Law University, Delhi, Seattle Law School and the University of Chicago Law School have supported our endeavours throughout and provided us with the community and collegiality required to undertake so mammoth a task. We want to thank C. Raj Kumar, vice chancellor of Jindal Global Law School, for his encouragement and helping make this book a reality.

The datasets used in this book are the product of years-long collective effort among teams at our various institutions. We would like to thank Malavika Parthasarathy who spent a year as a Research Fellow at the Centre for Constitutional Law, Policy and Governance, National Law University, Delhi, conducting research for this book. The National Law University, Delhi (NLU Delhi) student team was brilliantly led over the years by Hemangini Kalra, Sucheta Roy, Sanya Kumar, Shweta Kabra and Kudrat Agrawal. Along with the team leaders, Anwesha Choudhary, Aarushi Mahajan, Shreya Raman and Malavika Parthasarathy hand-coded the bulk of the cases and reviewed the entire dataset for errors and consistency. Devdutta Mukhopadhya and Tishta Tandon (NLU Delhi), and Lakshmi T. Nambiar, Rushil Batra and Manpreet Dhillon (NLSIU Bengaluru) provided us with excellent research assistance. Research professionals at the Coase-Sandor Institute at the University of Chicago Law School including Morgen Miller, Rafeh Qureshi, Jake Kramer and Dylan Baker provided extensive data processing and analysis. Special thanks go to Kyle Rozema, who contributed invaluable expertise in this data-gathering process. Consultation with the legal tech firm Provakil assisted our data-gathering efforts. Devanshi Saxena, Akanksha Gautam, Anurag Goswami and Vanya Chhabra also contributed to the project.

We thank Chirag Thakkar and Aparna Abhijit at Penguin Random House India for their patient and thoughtful shepherding of our manuscript through to publication.

Our families, especially our partners and our children (some of whom are younger than this project!), have been our support systems and generously shared us with our work. This project was made possible, and enriched in countless ways, by so many individuals and institutions that we cannot name them all here. We are grateful to all of them.

Notes

Introduction

1. See George Gadbois, 'Supreme Court Decision-making', *Banaras Law Journal* 10 (1974); V. R. Krishna Iyer, *Our Courts on Trial* 18 (1987). This assessment has been widely echoed in subsequent academic works on the Indian Supreme Court. See e.g., Shylashri Shankar, 'India's Judiciary: Imperium in Imperio?', *Routledge Handbook Of South Asian Politics* 165 (2010), ed. Paul Brass; Alexander Fischer, 'Higher Lawmaking as a Political Resource', *Sovereignty And Diversity* 186 (2008), ed. Miodrag Jovanović and Kristin Henrard.

2. 'Abolish Two Judge Benches: Fali Nariman', *Indian Express*, 10 April 2014.

3. See Supreme Court of India, http://supremecourtofindia.nic.in/outtoday/ Social%20 Justice%20Bench.pdf (notice issued by the Supreme Court on establishing the social justice bench); Utkarsh Anand, 'Allocate more time to Social Justice Bench, say experts,' *Indian Express*, 13 December 2014.

4. See Law Commission of India, *229th Report On Need For Division Of The Supreme Court Into A Constitution Bench At Delhi And Cassation Benches In Four Regions At Delhi, Chennai/Hyderabad, Kolkata And Mumbai*, August 2009, http://lawcommissionofindia.nic.in/ reports/report229.pdf.

5. Ibid.

6. See eg, The Constitution (Ninety Ninth) Amendment Act, 2014 and the National Judicial Appointments Commission Act, 2014.

7. *Asok Pande v. Supreme Court of India*, (2018) 5 SCC 341; *Shanti Bhushan v. Supreme Court of India*, (2018) 8 SCC 396.

8. Exceptions include George Gadbois, who, in the early days of the Indian Supreme Court, used quantitative empirical methods to study the Court. See eg, George Gadbois, 'Indian Judicial Behaviour', 5(3) *Economic and Political Weekly* 149 (1970); George Gadbois, 'Supreme Court Decision Making',10 *Banaras Law Journal* Article 1 (1974). More recently, Nick Robinson has contributed significantly to understanding broader structural issues about the Court through empirical methods. See eg, Nick Robinson, 'Structure Matters: The Impact of Court Structure on the Indian and U.S. Supreme Courts', 61 (1) *American Journal of Comparative Law* 173 (2013); Nick Robinson, 'A Quantitative Analysis of the Indian Supreme Court's Workload', 10 *Journal of Empirical Legal Studies* 570 (2013); Nick Robinson, et al., 'Interpreting the Constitution: Supreme Court Constitution Benches since Independence', 46(9) *Economic and Political Weekly* 27 (2011). In the last few years, Indian legal think-tanks such as Daksh and Vidhi Centre for Legal Policy have also created databases and used data to inform approaches to structural reform of the judiciary.

9. Supreme Court of India, *Annual Report 2018-2019*, 58 (2019), https://main.sci.gov.in/pdf/AnnualReports/Supreme_High_Court_AR_English_2018-19.pdf [hereinafter *Annual Report 2019*].

10. Constitution of India, Article 141.

11. Article 32 guarantees the right to move the Supreme Court for enforcement of fundamental rights. The Supreme Court also has original jurisdiction with respect to inter-state disputes and over certain election matters. Constitution of India, arts. 131 and 71. The President may also refer any matter to the Court for its advisory (non-binding) opinion. Constitution of India, art. 143.

12. Constituent Assembly Debates, Volume VII, 9 December 1948.

13. See Aparna Chandra, William H.J. Hubbard and Sital Kalantry, 'The Supreme Court of India: An Empirical Overview of the Institution', Table 2.2, *A Qualified Hope: The Indian Supreme Court and Progressive Social Change*, ed. Gerald N. Rosenberg and Sudhir Krishnaswamy (Cambridge: Cambridge University Press, 2019).

14. *S.P. Gupta v. Union of India*, AIR 1982 SC 149. The court's own data reveals, however, that even among cases admitted for merits hearing, PILs constitute only 1 per cent of the Court's cases (though, of course, given the complex nature of many PILs, they may take up a significant proportion of

the Court's time and resources). Nick Robinson, 'A Quantitative Analysis of the Indian Supreme Court's Workload', 10 *Journal of Empirical Legal Studies* 570, 590 (2013).

15. Aparna Chandra, William H.J. Hubbard and Sital Kalantry, 'The Supreme Court of India: An Empirical Overview of the Institution', Table 2.1, *A Qualified Hope: The Indian Supreme Court and Progressive Social Change*, ed. Gerald N. Rosenberg and Sudhir Krishnaswamy (Cambridge: Cambridge University Press, 2019).

16. Constitution of India, arts. 132, 133, 134. Although the Court's jurisdiction can be invoked through procuring a certificate of appeal from the high court, this practice is rarely used. One possible reason for the low use of the 'Certificate of Appeal' jurisdiction is that while ordinarily a petitioner has ninety days to file an SLP, the limitation for filing an SLP after the high court has refused a certificate of appeal is sixty days. Some experts suggested during interviews and interactions with us that lawyers do not invoke the certificate of appeal process so as to give themselves more time to file in the Supreme Court.

17. See list in *Annual Report 2019*, *supra* note 11, at 58.

18. *Kunhayammed v. State of Kerala* (2000) 6 SCC 359, 371 ('Article 136 of the Constitution is a special jurisdiction conferred on the Supreme Court which is sweeping in its nature. It is a residuary power in the sense that it confers an appellate jurisdiction on the Supreme Court subject to the special leave being granted in such matters as may not be covered by the preceding articles. It is an overriding provision conferring a special jurisdiction providing for invoking of the appellate jurisdiction of the Supreme Court not fettered by the sweep of preceding articles. Article 136 opens with a non-obstante clause and conveys a message that even in the field covered by the preceding articles, jurisdiction conferred by Article 136 is available to be exercised in an appropriate case').

19. *Pritam Singh v. State* AIR 1950 SC 169.

20. As the Court itself has stated, it has the power to interfere 'even with findings of fact . . . [as for example when] the acquittal is based on an irrelevant ground, or where the High Court allows itself to be deflected by red herrings drawn across the track, or where the evidence accepted by the trial court is rejected by the High Court after a perfunctory consideration, or where the baneful approach of the High Court has resulted in vital and crucial evidence being ignored, or for any such adequate reason, this Court may feel obliged to step in to secure the interests of justice, to appease the judicial conscience,

as it were.' *Arunachalam v. P.S.R. Sadanatham* (1979) 2 SCC 297, 300. See also, *Subedar v. State of U.P.* AIR 1971 SC 125.

21. See Chapter 2.
22. Aparna Chandra, William H.J. Hubbard and Sital Kalantry, 'The Supreme Court of India: A People's Court?', 1 *Indian Law Review* 145 (2017).
23. Ibid., Table 2.
24. Tarunabh Khaitan, 'The Indian Supreme Court's Identity Crisis: A Constitutional Court or a Court of Appeals?', 4 (1) *Indian Law Review* 1 (2020).
25. AIR 1950 SC 27.
26. Nick Robinson, et al., 'Interpreting the Constitution: Indian Supreme Court Constitution Benches Since Independence', 46 *Economic and Political Weekly* 27, (2011); George Gadbois, *Supreme Court of India: The Beginnings* (Oxford: Oxford University Press, 2017), pp. 88–89.
27. *Annual Report 2019*, supra note 11, at 80.
28. George H. Gadbois, Jr., 'The Supreme Court of India: A Preliminary Report of an Empirical Study', 4 *Journal of Constitutional & Parliamentary Studies* 34 (1970).
29. Constitution of India, art. 124 (1).
30. *Annual Report 2019*, *supra* note 11, at 81. The Court averaged 60,184 admissions matters per year for the period 2014–2018, both inclusive, for which the full year's data was available. Notably, the number of matters for admission has dropped significantly since 2017. It is not clear whether this is the result of a change in how cases are counted, the start of a new trend, or a temporary blip.
31. The Supreme Court of India website records an average of 960 judgments for the period 2015–2019, both inclusive, ranging from 920 judgments in 2015 to 1369 judgments in 2019.
32. Constitution of India, art. 145 (3).
33. (2014) 1 SCC 1.
34. (2016) 7 SCC 221.
35. Robinson, 'Interpreting the Constitution', *supra* note 8.
36. See Aparna Chandra, William H.J. Hubbard and Sital Kalantry, 'The Supreme Court of India: A People's Court?', Table 1.1 *Indian Law Review* 145 (2017).
37. Constitution of India, arts. 141, 144.
38. *Central Board of Dawoodi Bohra Community v. State of Maharashtra*, (2005) 2 SCC 673.
39. (2014) 3 SCC 183.

40. *Delhi Development Authority v. Sukhbir Singh*, (2016) 16 SCC 258.
41. *Indore Development Authority v. Shailendra*, (2018) 1 SCC 733.
42. (2018) 3 SCC 412.
43. *Indore Development Authority v. Manoharlal*, (2020) 8 SCC 129.
44. See Law Commission of India, *262nd Report on the Death Penalty*, Chapter 5 (2015); Usha Ramanathan, 'Of Life and Death', Seminar (2016).
45. Nick Robinson, 'The Structure and Functioning of the Supreme Court of India' in *A Qualified Hope: The Indian Supreme Court and Progressive Social Change*.
46. Court date upon court date. This is a line from a famous Bollywood movie, *Damini* (1993), where a lawyer, angry at the delays in the judicial system, vents his frustration at the Court and says (translated from Hindi) 'date upon date, all that I get from the Court is another date, I don't get justice.'
47. National Judicial Data Grid, https://njdg.ecourts.gov.in/njdgnew/index.php, last accessed 6 June 2020.
48. Ibid.
49. See Law Commission of India, *245th Report on Arrears and Backlog: Creating Additional Judicial (Wo)Manpower* (2014).
50. Constitution of India, art. 226.
51. National Judicial Data Grid, *supra* note 47, last accessed 8 June 2020.
52. This information is based on our data on pending cases in the Supreme Court Cases Dataset.
53. The bulk of the cases in the Supreme Court are dismissed *in limine*. To get a sense of delays in the Supreme Court, all *ex parte* disposals have been excluded. Only those cases where both parties are represented, have been included here. This provides a rough estimation of the time taken by the Court to dispose cases that it deems worthy of a closer scrutiny. Some of these cases are disposed at the after notice/final disposal stage and others are disposed after a full merits hearing.
54. In our dataset of hand-coded cases, we only had 123 cases that provided sufficient details of the procedural history of the case to be able to make this claim. Though we found nothing in these cases to make them as exceptional, we make our claims on the average time taken across the tiers of the judicial system based on limited data.
55. Aparna Chandra, William H.J. Hubbard and Sital Kalantry, 'The Supreme Court of India: An Empirical Overview of the Institution', *supra* note 15.
56. *Annual Report 2019*, *supra* note 5, at 81. (As per the record keeping practices of the Supreme Court, once the Court decided whether to admit a matter or

not, the case is considered disposed of as an admission matter. Those cases that are admitted, are considered as institutions under the head of regular matters. Thus, the ratio of instituted regular matters in a given year and the disposed admission matters in that same year gives us the Court's admission rate. The total number of institutions of regular matters in the period 2015–2019 (up to October, 2019) was 32,380. The total number of disposals of admission matters was 2,53,154. This translates to a 12.8 per cent admission rate.

57. *Supreme Court of India, Practice and Procedure: A Handbook of Information,* 102–104 (2017).

58. Rahul Hemrajani and Himanshu Agarwal, 'A Temporal Analysis of the Supreme Court of India's Workload' 3 *Indian Law Review* 125, 148 (2019)

59. *Kesavananda Bharati v. State of Kerala,* (1973) 4 SCC 225.

60. Upendra Baxi, 'The Judiciary as a Resource for Indian Democracy', *Seminar,* November 2010; *The Shifting Scales of Justice: The Supreme Court in Neo-liberal India,* ed. Mayur Suresh & Siddharth Narrain (2014).

61. Order VI, Rule 2, Supreme Court Rules, 2013. See also *Central Board of Dawoodi Bohra Community v. State of Maharashtra,* (2005) 2 SCC 673, 682.

62. The Chief Justice also assigns cases to Constitution Benches in certain other instances. For example, all References by the President under Article 143 of the Constitution are also posted before Constitution Benches. As per Order XLVI of the Supreme Court Rules, 2013, all petitions that question the election of the President and Vice-President under Article 71 of the Constitution read with Part III of the Presidential and Vice-Presidential Elections Act, 1952, shall be posted before a bench of five Judges.

63. Notice of Motion for Presenting an Address to the President of India for the Removal of Mr Justice Dipak Misra, Chief Justice of India, under Article 217 read with Article 124 (4) of the Constitution of India, available at http://www.lawyerscollective.org/wp-content/uploads/2018/04/watermarked_impeachment-motion-dipak-misra.pdf.

64. See generally, Benjamin Cardozo, *The Nature of the Judicial Process* (New Haven: Yale University Press, 1921).

65. Constitution of India, art. 124.

66. Law Commission of India, *14th Report on Reforms of the Judicial Administration,* volume 1, 34 (1958).

67. *Supreme Court Advocates-on-Record Association v. Union of India,* (2016) 5 SCC 1.

68. Jayant Sriram, 'The Controversy Around Justice Ranjan Gogoi's Rajya Sabha Nomination' *The Hindu,* 18 March 2020, https://www.thehindu.

com/podcast/the-controversy-around-justice-ranjan-gogois-rajya-sabha-nomination-the-hindu-in-focus-podcast/article31100747.ece.

69. Madhav S. Aney, Shubhankar Dam and Giovanni Ko, 'Jobs for Justice(s): Corruption in the Supreme Court of India', 64(3) *Journal of Law and Economics* 479 (2021).

70. Aparna Chandra, William H.J. Hubbard and Sital Kalantry, 'The Supreme Court of India: An Empirical Overview of the Institution', *supra* note 15; Aparna Chandra, William Hubbard and Sital Kalantry, 'From Executive Appointment to the Collegium System: The Impact on Diversity in the Indian Supreme Court', 51 *Vrü [Verfassung Und Recht In Übersee]* 273 (2018), https://doi.org/10.5771/0506-7286-2018-3-273); Aparna Chandra, William H.J. Hubbard and Sital Kalantry, 'The Supreme Court of India: A People's Court?' 1 *Indian Law Review* 145 (2017).

71. Earlier versions of the Supreme Court Opinions Dataset are described in, and were used in, Aparna Chandra, William H. J. Hubbard and Sital Kalantry (2017), 'The Supreme Court of India: A People's Court?', *Indian Law Review,* DOI: 10.1080/24730580.2017.1405583; Aparna Chandra, William H. J. Hubbard and Sital Kalantry (2019), 'The Supreme Court of India: An Empirical Overview of the Institution', *supra* note 15.

72. The Supreme Court Justices Dataset (along with the high court chief justices dataset) is described in, and was used in, Aparna Chandra, William H. J. Hubbard and Sital Kalantry (2018), 'From Executive Appointment to the Collegium System: The Impact on Diversity in the Indian Supreme Court', 51(3) *VRÜ [Verfassung und Recht in Übersee]* 273, https://doi.org/10.5771/0506-7286-2018-3-273.

73. Ibid.

Chapter 1: A 'People's Court'?

1. *Bihar Legal Support Society v. Chief Justice of India*, AIR 1987 SC 38.

2. Constitution of India, Article 32.

3. Upendra Baxi, 'Taking Suffering Seriously: Social Action Litigation in the Supreme Court of India' (1985) 4(1) *Third World Legal Studies* 107.

4. See e.g., Mayur Suresh and Siddharth Narrain, eds, *The Shifting Scales of Justice: The Supreme Court in Neo-liberal India* (New Delhi: Orient BlackSwan, 2014); Prashant Bhushan, 'Supreme Court and PIL: Changing Perspectives under Liberalization', 39 (18) *Economic and Political Weekly* 1770 (2004).

5. Usha Ramanathan, 'In the Name of the People: The Expansion of Judicial Power', *The Shifting Scales of Justice: The Supreme Court in Neo-liberal India.*

6. See e.g., Varun Gauri, 'Public Interest Litigation in India: Overreaching or Underachieving?' (2009) *World Bank Policy Research Working Paper No 5109*, 13, http://documents.worldbank.org/curated/en/675001468042007347/ pdf/WPS5109.pdf; Shylashri Shankar, *Scaling Justice, India's Supreme Court, Anti-Terror Laws, and Social Rights* (New Delhi: Oxford University Press, 2009).

7. Balakrishnan Rajagopal, 'Pro-Human Rights but Anti-Poor? A Critical Evaluation of the Indian Supreme Court from a Social Movement Perspective' 18 *Human Rights Review* 157 (2007), 166–68.

8. Manoj Mate, 'Globalization, Rights, and Judicial Review in the Supreme Court of India' 25 *Washington International Law Journal* 643 (2016).

9. Varun Gauri, 'Public Interest Litigation in India: Overreaching or Underachieving?'.

10. Sudhir Krishnaswamy and Madhav Khosla, 'Social Justice and the Supreme Court', *The Shifting Scales of Justice: The Supreme Court in Neo-Liberal India*, 109, 110.

11. Our analysis draws from the hit-rate methodology developed in empirical scholarship on racial profiling. The best-known paper on this method is John Knowles, Nicola Persico and Petra Todd, 'Racial Bias in Motor Vehicle Searches: Theory and Evidence', 109 *Journal of Political Economy* 203 (2001). Notable critiques and extensions include Dhammika Dharmapala and Stephen L. Ross, 'Racial Bias in Motor Vehicle Searches: Additional Theory and Evidence', 3 *The B.E. Journal of Economic Analysis & Policy* 1 (2004), and Shamena Anwar and Hanming Fang, 'An Alternative Test of Racial Prejudice in Motor Vehicle Searches: Theory and Evidence', 96 *American Economic Review* 127 (2006). See also Nicola Persico, 'Racial Profiling? Detecting Bias Using Statistical Evidence', 1 *Annual Review of Economics* 229 (2009), for a review.

12. See Nick Robinson, 'A Quantitative Analysis of the Indian Supreme Court's Workload', 10 *Journal of Empirical Legal Studies* (2013) 570, 598.

13. Supreme Court of India, *Annual Report 2014*, 76–79 (average of cases filed in 2010–14).

14. Article 136 of the Constitution permits the Court to grant, at its discretion, 'special leave to appeal from any judgment, decree, determination, sentence or order in any cause or matter passed or made by any court or tribunal in the territory of India'. The Court affirmed the broad scope of SLP jurisdiction in *Kunhayammed v. State of Kerala* (2000) 6 SCC 359.

15. We acknowledge that different judges may be guided by different goals and may also have differing abilities in error spotting. Thus, we do not assume that every judge approaches SLPs with the same approach or every judge is equally strict. Our approach does rely on some important assumptions, however. First, we assume that all case categories have comparable fractions of petitions raising egregious errors versus petitions raising less obvious errors (which the Court still wants to correct, if it spots them). Second, we assume that a settlement is rare in the Supreme Court. Anecdotally, experienced litigators before the Supreme Court have informed us that relatively few cases settle after admission.

16. See Table 4, Panel B in Aparna Chandra, William H. J. Hubbard and Sital Kalantry, 'The Supreme Court of India: A People's Court?', *Indian Law Review* (2017), DOI: 10.1080/24730580.2017.1405583.

17. Ibid., Table 4, Panel A.

18. Ibid., Table 5.

19. Supreme Court of the United States, 'Frequently Asked Questions (FAQ)', https://www.supremecourt.gov/faq.aspx (answering 'How many cases are appealed to the court each year and how many cases does the Court hear?' with 'The Court receives approximately 7,000–8,000 petitions for a writ of *certiorari* each term. The Court grants and hears oral argument in about 80 cases.').

20. Rahul Hemrajani and Himanshu Agarwal, 'A temporal analysis of the Supreme Court of India's workload', 3(2), *Indian Law Review* 125-158 (2019), DOI: 10.1080/24730580.2019.163751.

21. See Table 3 in Aparna Chandra, William H. J. Hubbard and Sital Kalantry, The Supreme Court of India: A People's Court?, *Indian Law Review* (2017), DOI: 10.1080/24730580.2017.1405583.

22. Hemrajani and Agarwal (2019).

23. Ibid. at 10. This is the median time. The mean (or average) time is a bit higher, around five or six minutes.

24. JUDIS, the official e-reporter of the Supreme Court of India records 900 judgments for 2014. For statistics on SLPs and appeals, see Table 1 in the ILR paper (The total number of opinions per year is greater than those listed in Table 1, due to cases within the Court's original jurisdiction). Note that the ten-page average length is inclusive of all opinions for a given case.

25. Andrew Green and Albert H. Yoon, 'Triaging the Law: Developing the Common Law on the Supreme Court of India', 14 *Journal of Empirical Legal Studies*, 683–715 (2017).

26. Ibid. at 701. Of course, we cannot know whether at some future date, a future decision will cite a past decision. But in their data, less than half of all decisions since 2000 have never been cited.
27. *Bihar Legal Support Society v. Chief Justice of India*, AIR 1987 SC 38.
28. *Y.S. Jagan Mohan Reddy v. CBI* (2013) 7 SCC 439.
29. This is not an isolated example. See, e.g., *Maruti Nivrutti Navale v. State of Maharashtra* (2012) 9 SCC 235; *Jignesh v. State of Gujarat* (2011) 10 SCC 591 (both pertaining to bail where the Court decided—without reference to or discussion of any prior law—whether, on the facts of the case, bail was warranted or not).
30. *Darshan Gupta v. Radhika Gupta* (2013) 9 SCC 1.
31. Law is cited once, however, in another part of the opinion. The only discussion on law took place when one party argued that despite the law not supporting divorce in the case, the Court should exercise its power to do 'complete justice' between parties (see Constitution of India, Art. 142) to dissolve the marriage in any case. This plea was rejected on the ground that the facts of the case were not suited to the exercise of such power by the Court.
32. Under Article 141 of the Constitution of India, law stated by the Supreme Court is binding on all courts.
33. Amrit Amirapu, 'Justice Delayed is Development Denied: The Effect of Slow Courts on Economic Outcomes in India', 26 August 2016, http://www.ideasforindia.in/article.aspx?article=Justice-delayed-is-development-denied-The-effect-of-slow-courts-on-economic-outcomes-in-India.
34. See Table 1 in Chandra, Hubbard and Kalantry (2017).
35. See generally Rishad Chowdhury, Note, 'Missing the Wood for the Trees: The Unseen Crisis in the Supreme Court' (2012) 5 *NUJS Law Review* 251; Nick Robinson, 'India's Judicial Architecture', *The Oxford Handbook of Indian Constitutional Law*, ed. Sujit Choudhry et al. (2016).
36. Abhinav Chandrachud, *Supreme Whispers: Conversations with the Judges of the Supreme Court of India*, chapter 3 (Gurgaon: PRHI, 2018).
37. It said that 'no effort should be made to restrict the powers of this Court under Article 136 because while exercising its powers under Article 136 of the Constitution of India, this Court can, after considering facts of the case to be decided, very well use its discretion'. *Mathai @ Joby v. George* (2016) SCC Online SC 410.
38. *Bihar Legal Support Society v. Chief Justice of India* AIR 1987 SC 38.

Chapter 2: Explosion, Exclusion, Evasion: The Burden of Backlogs

1. National Judicial Data Grid, https://njdg.ecourts.gov.in/njdgnew/index. php, last accessed 6 June 2020.

2. National Judicial Data Grid (High Courts of India), https://njdg.ecourts. gov.in/hcnjdgnew/, last accessed 8 June 2020.

3. Article 226. For a discussion on the scope of the writ jurisdiction under Article 226, see *Ramakrishna Mission v. Kago Kunya*, (2019) 16 SCC 303.

4. National Judicial Data Grid, last accessed 8 June 2020.

5. For example, at the National Consultation for Strengthening the Judiciary towards Reducing Pendency and Delays, the then minister for law and justice, M. Veerappa Moily, presented a vision statement to the Chief Justice of India, encapsulating the government's vision and action plan for reducing delays. The recommendations were all geared towards the delay and arrears reduction in the trial courts and the high courts, available at https://doj.gov. in/sites/default/files/Vision-Statement_0_0.pdf, last accessed 8 June 2020. This document formed the basis for the working of the National Mission for Justice Delivery and Legal Reforms, a mission mode project for inter alia, reduction of delays in the judicial system. The focus of the national mission's work has also been on lower courts. Details of the National Mission for Justice Delivery and Legal Reforms are available at https://doj.gov.in/ national-mission-justice-delivery-and-legal-reforms, last accessed 8 June 2020.

6. Nick Robinson, 'A Quantitative Analysis of the Indian Supreme Court's Workload', 10 *Journal of Empirical Legal Studies* 570, 574 (2013), p. 3.

7. The bulk of the cases in the Supreme Court are dismissed *in limine*, that is, at the very threshold without even issuing notice to the other party. When the court decides to take a closer look, it issues notice to the other side to appear before it. To get a sense of backlog in the Supreme Court, all *ex parte* disposals—where the other party has not been asked to appear—have been excluded. Only those cases where both parties are represented have been included here. This provides a rough estimation of the time taken by the Court to dispose cases that it deems worthy of a closer scrutiny. Some of these cases are disposed at the after notice/final disposal stage, and others are disposed after a full merits hearing.

8. Our data does not independently record whether a case was disposed at the admissions stage, at the final disposal stage, or after a regular hearing. However, we do record which cases were disposed *ex parte*. *Ex parte* disposals

commonly occur only at admissions when a case is dismissed *in limine* (see ibid). We have excluded all *ex parte* decisions from our calculations to arrive at a rough estimate of the cases that crossed the admissions threshold. However, our approach is likely to undercount cases disposed at the admissions stage in two respects. First, if the Court finds that there is some merit to the appeal, it generally issues notice to the other side to appear and explain why the matter should not be admitted. Once the other side appears, the matter may still be dismissed at the admissions stage. Second, anticipating the other side will appeal, a party can file a caveat in the Court, asking that the matter should not be listed for admissions without giving such party a chance to be heard. In such a case, the other side will be represented even at the initial admissions stage. For that reason, even an initial admissions hearing may not be decided *ex parte*. These sorts of cases, though dismissed at the admissions stage, might still make it into our data of admitted matters. If that is the case, our data under-reports the time lapse—and therefore the problem of delay in the Supreme Court. As a result, the fastest cases might take longer than reported by us.

9. In our dataset of hand-coded cases, we only had 123 cases that provided sufficient details of the procedural history of the case to be able to make this claim. Though we found nothing in these cases to deem them as exceptional, we make our claims on the average time taken across the tiers of the judicial system based on limited data. However, our data matches that of other studies. See, for e.g., Tarunabh Khaitan, 'The Indian Supreme Court's Identity Crisis: A Constitutional Court or a Court of Appeals?' 4:1, *Indian Law Review* 1 (2020).

10. See Chandra, Hubbard and Kalantry, 'The Supreme Court of India: An Empirical Overview of the Institution' *A Qualified Hope: The Indian Supreme Court and Progressive Social Change* 43–76 (2019), ed. G. Rosenberg, S. Krishnaswamy and S. Bail.

11. Article 145, Constitution of India.

12. See Supreme Court of India, Indian Judiciary: Annual Report 2020-2021, p. 84, https://main.sci.gov.in/pdf/AnnualReports/12012022_114003.pdf, last accessed 17 April 2023.

13. This data is from our dataset of information scraped from the Supreme Court website, which shows that of the 1,52,720 cases pending on 3 November 2018, 1,17,042 cases involved Civil and Criminal Appeals, SLPs and Criminal Miscellaneous Petitions. The data excludes 34,229 cases for which we did not have case type information, from this count.

14. Aparna Chandra, William H. J. Hubbard and Sital Kalantry, 'The Supreme Court of India: A People's Court?', 2:1 *Indian Law Review* 145 (2017).

15. Nick Robinson, 'A Quantitative Analysis of the Indian Supreme Court's Workload', 10 *Journal of Empirical Legal Studies* 570, 574 (2013).

16. See Chandra, Hubbard and Kalantry, 'The Supreme Court of India: An Empirical Overview of the Institution' *A Qualified Hope: The Indian Supreme Court and Progressive Social Change* 43–76 (2019), ed. G. Rosenberg, S. Krishnaswamy and S. Bail, (Table 2).

17. See Aparna Chandra, William H. J. Hubbard and Sital Kalantry, 'The Supreme Court of India: A People's Court?', 2:1 *Indian Law Review* 145 (2017), Table 2 (dealing with admitted matters).

18. Calculated using data in the Supreme Court of India, Indian Judiciary: *Annual Report 2018-2019*, pp. 81, 85. In the time period 2014–2018 for which data is available for the full year, 3,00,921 cases were filed for admission in the Supreme Court. Of these, 1747 were PIL related writ petitions, comprising both civil and criminal matters and included 9 *suo moto* PILs. This implies that only 0.6 per cent of the admissions docket comprises PILs. This figure does not include the tens of thousands of letter petitions received by the Supreme Court, but which rarely make it onto the Court's docket. As per data gathered from the Supreme Court website, 7633 cases were categorized by the Court registry as PIL matters. This also amounts to 0.6 per cent of the entire docket as available on the Supreme Court's website.

19. See Chandra, Hubbard and Kalantry, 'The Supreme Court of India: An Empirical Overview of the Institution' *A Qualified Hope: The Indian Supreme Court and Progressive Social Change*, ed. G. Rosenberg, S. Krishnaswamy and S. Bail (Cambridge: Cambridge University Press, 2019), pp. 43–76 (Table 1).

20. Our dataset of information scraped from the Supreme Court website shows that matters categorized by the registry as PIL and Letter Petition matters (n=4104) took, on average, 1107 days between filing and disposal.

21. Rahul Hemrajani and Himanshu Agarwal, 'A Temporal Analysis of the Supreme Court of India's Workload' 3 *Indian Law Review* 125, 148 (2019).

22. Supreme Court of India, *Annual Report 2018–2019* (2019) 81, https://main.sci.gov.in/pdf/AnnualReports/Supreme_High_Court_AR_English_2018-19.pdf. (As per the record keeping practices of the Supreme Court, once the court decided whether to admit a matter or not, the case is considered disposed of as an admission matter. Those cases that are admitted, are considered as fresh institutions under the head of regular matters. Thus,

the ratio of instituted regular matters in a given year and the disposed admission matters in that same year gives us the court's admission rate. The total number of institutions of regular matters in the period 2015–2019 (up to October 2019) was 32,380. The total number of disposals of admission matters was 2,53,154. This translates to a 12.8 per cent admission rate.

23. Parties who expect that an appeal may be filed in the Supreme Court against an order of a lower court or tribunal, can file a caveat with the registry. If such a caveat has been filed, the registry will not list the matter for admission without giving notice to the caveator.

24. Supreme Court of India, *Practice and Procedure: A Handbook of Information* (2017), 102–104. On details of the 'after notice' or 'final disposal' stage, see Jahnavi Sindhu and Vikram Aditya Narayan, 'Institution Matters: A Critical Analysis of the Role of the Supreme Court of India and the Responsibilities of the Chief Justice' (2018) 51:3 *Verfassung und Recht in Übersee/Law and Politics in Africa, Asia and Latin America,* 290–331.

25. Nick Robinson et al., 'Interpreting the Constitution: Supreme Court Constitution Benches since Independence', 16 (9) *Economic and Political Weekly* 27 (2011).

26. See Chandra, Hubbard and Kalantry, 'The Supreme Court of India: An Empirical Overview of the Institution' *A Qualified Hope: The Indian Supreme Court and Progressive Social Change* 43–76 (2019), ed. G. Rosenberg, S. Krishnaswamy and S. Bail. (Table 15).

27. (2014) 1 SCC 1.

28. See Order VI, Rule 1, Supreme Court Rules 2013 (as amended in 2019).

29. Nick Robinson, 'Structure Matters: The Impact of Court Structure on the Indian and U.S. Supreme Courts' (2013) 61:1 *American Journal of Comparative Law* 173.

30. *Pritham Singh v. State,* AIR 1950 SC 169; *State of Bombay v. Rusy Mistry,* AIR 1960 SC 391; *Chandi Prasad Chokhani v. State of Bihar,* AIR 1961 SC 1708; *Jamshed Hormusji Wadia v. Board of Trustees,* Port of Mumbai AIR 2004 SC 1815.

31. *Pritham Singh v. State,* AIR 1950 SC 169; *State of Bombay v. Rusy Mistry,* AIR 1960 SC 391.

32. *Arunachalam v. P.S.R. Sadanatham,* (1979) 2 SCC 297; *Jamshed Hormusji Wadia v. Board of Trustees, Port of Mumbai,* AIR 2004 SC 1815. *Municipal Board, Pratabgarh v. Mahendra Singh Chawla,* (1982) 3 SCC 331; *Chandra Singh v. State of Rajasthan,* AIR 2003 SC 2889.

33. *Arunachalam v. P. S. R. Sadhanantham,* AIR 1979 SC 1284.

34. *Mathai @ Joby v. George*, (2010) 4 SCC 358

35. *Mathai @ Joby v. George*, (2016) 7 SCC 700.

36. Andrew Green and Albert Yoon, 'Triaging the Law: Developing the Common Law on the Supreme Court of India', 14 *Journal of Empirical Legal Studies* 683 (2017).

37. As Nick Robinson notes, this argument is often advanced in support of a wide SLP jurisdiction. Nick Robinson, 'Structure Matters: The Impact of Court Structure on the Indian and U.S. Supreme Courts' (2013) 61:1 *American Journal of Comparative Law 173.*

38. See e.g., 'T. R. Andhyarujina, Restoring the Supreme Court's Exclusivity', *The Hindu*, 21 August 2013, https://www.thehindu.com/opinion/lead/Restoring-the-Supreme-Court%E2%80%99s-exclusivity/article11557294.ece, (a senior and very respected member of the Bar making this argument).

39. See, Aparna Chandra, William H. J. Hubbard & Sital Kalantry, 'The Supreme Court of India: A People's Court?, 2:1 *Indian Law Review* 145 (2017).

40. *Imtiyaz Ahmad v. State of UP*, (2012) 2 SCC 688.

41. H.M. Seervai, *Constitutional Law of India* (4th Edition, 2013), pp. 2964–65.

42. We have counted all cases that were not decided *ex parte* as cases where notice was issued. This includes cases where a caveat was filed. The number therefore likely underrepresents how long cases take after notice is issued.

43. See Chandra, Hubbard and Kalantry, 'The Supreme Court of India: An Empirical Overview of the Institution', *supra* note 26.

44. Jahnavi Sindhu and Vikram Aditya Narayan, 'Institution Matters: A Critical Analysis of the Role of the Supreme Court of India and the Responsibilities of the Chief Justice', 51:3 (2018) *Verfassung und Recht in Übersee/Law and Politics in Africa, Asia and Latin America,* 290–331.

45. 'Something Fundamentally Wrong' with SC Registry, Says CJI Gogoi', The Quint, 25 July 2019, https://www.thequint.com/news/india/cji-ranjan-gogoi-irked-over-non-listing-of-urgent-cases-says-something-fundamentally-wrong-with-sc-registry.

46. *Reepak Kansal v. Secretary General*, Supreme Court of India, 2020 SCC Online SC 558.

47. Ibid.

48. Radhika Roy, 'J&K Govt Extends Internet Restrictions Even As SC Directions For Review By "Special Committee" Await Compliance', LiveLaw, 8 July 2020, https://www.livelaw.in/top-stories/jk-govt-extends-

internet-restrictions-even-as-sc-directions-for-review-by-special-committee-await-compliance-159601>

49. Gautam Bhatia, 'A Tale of Evasion, Deference and Inconsistency', *Hindustan Times*, 10 December 2020, https://www.hindustantimes.com/columns/a-tale-of-evasion-deference-and-inconsistency/story-uPCbRzn40SLooj6mVLbpOJ.html.

50. *Puttaswamy II v. Union of India*, (2019) 1 SCC 1.

51. *Association For Democratic Reforms v. Union of India*, 2019 SCC Online SC 1878.

52. *Association for Democratic Reforms v. Union of India*, 2021 SCC Online SC 266.

53. See discussion in Chapter 5.

54. See Rahul Hemrajani and Himanshu Agarwal (2019), 'A temporal analysis of the Supreme Court of India's workload, *Indian Law Review*', 3:2, 125–158 (explaining how setting up Constitution Benches has the effect of increasing case disposal times across the board).

55. *Mathai @ Joby v. George,* (2010) 4 SCC 358.

56. Ibid.

57. Ibid.

58. Ibid.

59. *Mathai @ Joby v. George,* (2016) 7 SCC 700.

60. Abhinav Chandrachud, *Supreme Whispers: Conversations with the Judges of the Supreme Court of India*, chapter 3.

61. See Article 137 read with Order XLVII, Supreme Court of India Rules, 2013.

62. Order XLVII, Rule 1 of the Supreme Court Rules, 2013. On the procedures that apply in a review petition, see *Mohd. Arif v. Registrar, Supreme Court of India*, (2014) 9 SCC 737.

63. *Kantaru Rajeevaru v. Indian Young Lawyers Assn*, (2020) 3 SCC 52.

64. See details in Chapter 4.

65. For a detailed discussion see, See Chandra, A., Hubbard, W., & Kalantry, S., 'The Supreme Court of India: An Empirical Overview of the Institution', *supra* note 26.

66. Note that the reversal rate for constitutional matters is 100 per cent due to there being only one observation with complete information on reversal.

67. See e.g., 'T. R. Andhyarujina, Restoring the Supreme Court's Exclusivity', *The Hindu*, 21 August 2013, https://www.thehindu.com/opinion/lead/Restoring-the-Supreme-Court%E2%80%99s-exclusivity/article11557294.

ece>; K. K. Venugopal, For a Proximate and Speedy Justice, *The Hindu*, 30 April 2010, https://www.thehindu.com/opinion/lead/For-proximate-and-speedy-justice/article16297745.ece.

68. *V. Vasanthakumar v. H.C. Bhatia*, (2016) 7 SCC 686 (petition to create a separate national court of appeals between the high courts and the Supreme Court).

Chapter 3: 'Face Value': The Power and Influence of Senior Advocates

1. Confidential interview, 14 January 2016.
2. For example, a news story noted that Vijay Sondhi, a law partner in New Delhi, has pointed out that senior advocates may 'simply be better prepared and have far more experience . . . arguing in court' than other lawyers, Alok Prasanna Kumar, 'The true worth of a senior advocate', livemint.com, 16 September 2015.
3. Marc Galanter and Nick Robinson, 'India's Grand Advocates: A Legal Elite Flourishing in the Era of Globalization', *International Journal of the Legal Profession*, 20:3, 241–265 (2013).
4. Ibid.
5. Prachi Shrivastava, 'Which 9 top lawyers easily charge Rs 15+ lakh per hearing? 42 Delhi seniors' fees revealed', Legally India, 8 September 2015, https://www.legallyindia.com/the-bench-and-the-bar/revealed-delhi-rsquo-s-top-advocates-won-rsquo-t-even-touch-your-case-for-less-than-rs-5-lakh-20150908-6555. Another study stated that in 2015 senior advocates earned between Rs 75,000 and 16.5 lakh per hearing in the Supreme Court. Alok Prasanna Kumar, 'The true worth of a senior advocate', livemint.com, 16 September 2015, https://www.livemint.com/Politics/FFgFOFnzN8rqvRNWTTgugM/The-true-worth-of-a-senior-advocate.html.
6. Galanter and Robinson, 'India's Grand Advocates', at 247.
7. 'While we're busy looking out for the highest paid celebrities in Bollywood, let us throw some light on the fact that our lawyers earn no less than any celebrity. India is home to some very influential and powerful lawyers who can hold the entire court in awe with their fabulous argument skills and yes, they charge a bomb for it!', '10 highest-paid lawyers in India', India TV, 6 April 2017, https://www.indiatvnews.com/lifestyle/news-these-are-the-10-highest-paid-lawyers-in-india-375827.
8. Ibid. A story from 2017 reported similar numbers, 'Meet India's men in black: 5 lawyers who charge a bomb for their expertise', *India Today*, 5 April

2017, https://www.indiatoday.in/fyi/story/india-biggest-lawyer-top-list-ram-jethamalani-harsh-salve-soli-j-sorabjee-969639-2017-04-05.

9. Galanter and Robinson, 'India's Grand Advocates', at 246.

10. Ibid. at 247.

11. Ibid.

12. Abhinav Chandrachud, *Supreme Whispers: Conversations with Judges of the Supreme Court of India 1980-89* (India Viking, 2018), p. 93 (describing George Gadbois' interview with judges in the 1980s).

13. Galanter and Robinson, 'India's Grand Advocates', at 247.

14. In our data on Supreme Court judges from 1993 (at the beginning of the Collegium) to 2019, the youngest age at appointment was fifty-five and the oldest was sixty-two.

15. In our data on Supreme Court justices from 1993 to 2019, the median age at appointment in our data is fifty-nine.

16. See *K. M. Nanavati vs. State of Maharashtra*, 1962 AIR 605, 1962 SCR Supl. (1) 567.

17. See Nick Robinson, 'A Quantitative Analysis of the Indian Supreme Court's Workload' 10 *Journal of Empirical Legal Studies* 570, 583 (2013). See also Chapter 2 on the Court as a 'people's court' for a longer discussion of SLPs.

18. Ibid.

19. Ibid.

20. Alok Prasanna Kumar, 'The true worth of a senior advocate', livemint.com, 16 September 2015.

21. 'A correlation between the appearance of senior advocates and success in getting an SLP admitted is not necessarily equal to causation by the senior tag itself', Alok Prasanna Kumar, 'The true worth of a senior advocate', livemint.com, 16 September 2015,

22. Andrew Green and Albert H. Yoon, 'Triaging the Law: Developing the Common Law on the Supreme Court of India', 14 *Journal of Empirical Legal Studies* 683 (2017). We discuss this study in more detail in Chapter 1 on the Court as a 'People's Court'.

23. These cases were all SLPs coded as 'ordinary civil matters' coming out of the Delhi High Court and filed in the Supreme Court in 2010 that we were able to collect from the Supreme Court website. We chose these criteria to ensure a sample of cases that were similar in terms of case type, origin and year but which varied in terms of representation by advocates and senior advocates. Each of these cases was hand-coded by our researcher Malavika Parthasarathy. Coding was completed on 21 April 2019.

24. See Aparna Chandra, William H. J. Hubbard and Sital Kalantry (2017), 'The Supreme Court of India: A People's Court?', *Indian Law Review* at 10 (DOI: 10.1080/24730580.2017.1405583).

25. We defined success as the Court admitting the petition or issuing notice. We defined failure as the Court dismissing the petition. We did not count other outcomes, such as withdrawn petitions, in this calculation (such outcomes were very rare). In addition to looking at outcomes at the initial admissions-stage hearings, we collected outcomes at subsequent admissions-stage hearings.

26. The breakdown by advocate type of subsequent admissions hearings, was 93 per cent success rate for petitions brought by senior advocates and 85 per cent success rate for petitions brought by other advocates.

27. For details on this data collection effort, see Chandra, Hubbard and Kalantry (2017).

28. Our data include 2570 petitioners represented by senior advocates (57.16 per cent win rate) and 2858 petitioners represented by advocates (59.90 per cent win rate). The difference in win rates is statistically significant at the 5 per cent level (two-tailed t-test).

29. We note that this pattern is the strongest for civil cases. In civil cases, advocates representing petitioners have a 66 per cent win rate in our data, as opposed to a 58 per cent win rate for senior advocates representing petitioners. For criminal cases, petitioners represented by senior advocates and by other advocates both win 54 per cent of the time. As we discuss in Chapter 1, we expect to see lower success rates for groups that receive preferential access from the Court for admission. This is because the Court will admit a weak case brought by a favoured litigant or lawyer even when it would not admit an equally weak case brought a disfavoured litigant or lawyer. In this way, favoured groups have more weak cases admitted, lowering their overall success rate.

30. See Chapter 1 for the complete discussion of these statistics.

31. Not unlike in India, legal news sources in the United States often report statistics about the small number of elite lawyers who handle a disproportionate amount of the cases argued in the Supreme Court. See, for example, Kimberly Strawbridge Robinson, 'SCOTUS Milestone: Clement Tops 100 High Court Arguments', *Bloomberg Law*, 21 February 2020, https://news.bloomberglaw.com/us-law-week/scotus-milestone-clement-tops-100-high-court-arguments. This story reports that Paul Clement, former United States solicitor general, is one of three lawyers in the twenty-

first century to reach the milestone of 100 oral arguments before the Supreme Court.

32. Information on the United States Supreme Court can be found at https://www.supremecourt.gov.

33. It said that 'no effort should be made to restrict the powers of this Court under Article 136 because while exercising its powers under Article 136 of the Constitution of India, this Court can, after considering facts of the case to be decided, very well use its discretion'. *Mathai @ Joby v. George* (2016) SCC OnLine SC 410.

Chapter 4: First Amongst Equals? Master of the Roster and Strategic Case Assignments

1. '"Democracy is in danger": Watch the historic press conference held by four Supreme Court judges', Scroll.in, 13 January 2018, https://scroll.in/video/864863/democracy-is-in-danger-watch-the-historic-press-conference-held-by-four-supreme-court-judges.

2. Ibid.

3. A copy of the letter is available at https://www.thehindubusinessline.com/multimedia/archive/03221/Judges_letter_to_C_3221033a.pdf.

4. *Campaign for Judicial Accountability and Reforms v. Union of India*, (2018) 1 SCC 196, p. 199.

5. *State of Rajasthan v. Prakash Chand*, (1998) 1 SCC 1, p. 39.

6. *Asok Pande v. Supreme Court of India*, (2018) 5 SCC 341, p. 351.

7. *Shanti Bhushan v. Supreme Court of India*, (2018) 8 SCC 396, p. 418.

8. *Asok Pande v. Supreme Court of India*, (2018) 5 SCC 341; *Shanti Bhushan v. Supreme Court of India*, (2018) 8 SCC 396.

9. This roster is available at https://main.sci.gov.in/judges-roster-0.

10. Order VI, Rule 2, Supreme Court Rules, 2013. See also *Central Board of Dawoodi Bohra Community v. State of Maharashtra*, (2005) 2 SCC 673, p. 682.

11. Article 145 (3), Constitution of India. All references by the President under Article 143 of the Constitution are also posted before Constitution Benches. As per Order XLVI of the Supreme Court Rules, 2013, all petitions that question the election of the President and Vice-President under Article 71 of the Constitution read with Part III of the Presidential and Vice-Presidential Elections Act, 1952, shall be posted before a bench of five judges.

12. The case-specific rostering power also comes into play in the case of review petitions under Article 137 of the Constitution. Are far as possible, a review

petition has to be heard by the same bench that passed the order that is now sought to be reviewed. However, if the judges on that bench are not available, for reasons of retirement or otherwise, the Chief Justice has to allocate the case to specific judges or benches. See Order XLVII, Supreme Court Rules, 2013.

13. See 'Imposition of Exemplary Costs on Petitioner Reignites Controversy Over Supreme Court's Role', The Wire, 3 December 2017, https://thewire.in/law/imposition-exemplary-costs-reignites-controversy-supreme-courts-role.

14. *Kamini Jaiswal v. Union of India*, (2018) 1 SCC 194.

15. *Campaign for Judicial Accountability and Reforms v. Union of India*, (2018) 1 SCC 196

16. *Asok Pande v. Supreme Court of India*, (2018) 5 SCC 341 : 2018 SCC OnLine SC 361.

17. *Shanti Bhushan v. Supreme Court of India*, (2018) 8 SCC 396 : 2018 SCC OnLine SC 669.

18. Nick Robinson et al., 'Interpreting the Constitution: Supreme Court Constitution Benches since Independence', 16 (9) *Economic and Political Weekly* 27, 28 (2011).

19. The number of judges increased from eight in 1950, to eleven in 1956, to fourteen in 1960, to eighteen in 1977, to twenty-six in 1986, to thirty-one in 2008, to thirty-four in 2019.

20. Nick Robinson et al., 'Interpreting the Constitution: Supreme Court Constitution Benches since Independence', 16 (9) *Economic and Political Weekly* 27 (2011).

21. This chapter focuses on how the Chief Justice allocates cases to judges. The Master of the Roster power also allows the Chief Justice to determine when a matter will be heard (by determining 'listing priorities' and by constituting a bench to hear a case). These issues are addressed in Chapter 2.

22. George Gadbois, 'Supreme Court Decision Making', 10 *Banaras Law Journal* Article 1 (1974).

23. Ibid. See also, George Gadbois, 'Indian Judicial Behaviour', 5(3) *Economic and Political Weekly* 149 (1970).

24. Abhinav Chandrachud, *Supreme Whispers: Conversations with Judges of the Supreme Court of India 1980-1989*, 20 (Gurgaon: PRHI, 2018).

25. See ibid., pp. 17–20.

26. Nick Robinson et al., 'Interpreting the Constitution: Supreme Court Constitution Benches since Independence', 16 (9) *Economic and Political Weekly* 27 (2011).

27. Krithika Ashok found that in the time period 1993–2016, Constitution Bench cases had a dissent rate of 16.7 per cent. Ashok notes that this overall rate of dissent masks widely varying rates of dissent year on year. She also notes that dissents are higher on larger benches—of seven, nine or eleven judges. In our own study, the dissent rate on Constitution Benches was 5.9 per cent, and in the time period of our study, the Court only handed down thirty-nine Constitution Bench decisions. Krithika Ashok, 'Disinclined to dissent? A study of the Supreme Court of India', 1 *Indian Law Review* 7–35 (2017).

28. Lee Epstein, William Landes and Richard Posner, *The Behavior of Federal Judges: A Theoretical and Empirical Study of Rational Choice* (Harvard University Press, 2013), p. 258.

29. Overall, 0.2 per cent of all votes cast by pusine judges (that is, judges other than the Chief Justice of India) and by Chief Justices respectively are dissenting votes. Note that this statistic counts each vote and not each case. In a bench of five judges for example, there will be five votes but only one case. If two judges dissent, then at a case level count, the case will count as one case featuring a dissent. However, at a vote level count, the case will count as three non-dissenting votes and two dissenting votes.

30. In the time period of our study, for benches of three or more judges, a bench headed by the Chief Justice was about twice as likely to see a dissent, as a bench without the Chief Justice (0.8 per cent vs. 0.4 per cent). Constitution Bench decisions in this period, where the Chief Justice was not part of the bench, were unanimous on the outcome—that is, there was no dissent in these cases.

31. Further, Chief Justices are not likely to predict with certainty how other judges will decide each case. A judge's decision often turns on the nature of arguments presented at the bar. Indeed, the entire judicial process would be a sham if the hearing in the case had no impact on the outcome of the case. For these reasons, no one can consistently predict with certainty before cases are even heard, how judges will rule on each case.

32. For three-judge benches: Seniority correlation of 0. 0.000236 to bench assignment; p value > .1; observations= 195. For 5+ judge benches: Seniority correlation of 0.00160 to bench assignment; p value > .1; observations =183.

33. Being the CJI increases the likelihood of appointment to the bench by 30 per cent.

34. Nick Robinson et al., 'Interpreting the Constitution: Supreme Court Constitution Benches since Independence', 16 (9) *Economic and Political Weekly* 27, 31 (2011).

35. Being the CJI increases the likelihood of appointment to the bench by 49 per cent.

36. See e.g., Manu Sebastian, 'Chief Justice of India Should Have No Power To Assign Cases To Benches, Allotment Must Be Automated: Dushyant Dave', LiveLaw, 11 August 2022 https://www.livelaw.in/top-stories/chief-justice-of-india-master-of-roster-power-to-assign-cases-to-bench-dushyant-dave-206289; Abhinav Chandrachud, *Supreme Whispers: Conversations with Judges of the Supreme Court of India 1980-1989*, 17–20 (Gurgaon: PRHI, 2018).

37. There are fifty-eight judges in our dataset. However, we have excluded Justice Tarun Chatterjee from our count because in the time period of our study, while he was on the bench, there were no Constitution Benches to be assigned to him.

38. See Shrutanjaya Bharadwaj, 'Constituting Constitution Benches of the Supreme Court: An Analysis', *Bar and Bench*, 28 September 2019, https://www.barandbench.com/columns/constituting-constitution-benches-of-the-supreme-court-an-analysis.

39. *Shayara Bano v. Union of India*, (2017) 9 SCC 1

40. Letter by Justices Chelameswar, Gogoi, Lokur and Joseph to Chief Justice Dipak Misra, https://www.thehindubusinessline.com/multimedia/archive/03221/Judges_letter_to_C_3221033a.pdf.

41. *Asok Pande v. Supreme Court of India*, (2018) 5 SCC 341; *Shanti Bhushan v. Supreme Court of India*, (2018) 8 SCC 396.

42. Notice of Motion for Presenting an Address to the President of India for the Removal of Mr. Justice Dipak Misra, Chief Justice of India, under Article 217 read with Article 124 (4) of the Constitution of India, http://www.lawyerscollective.org/wp-content/uploads/2018/04/watermarked_impeachment-motion-dipak-misra.pdf.

43. Order of the Chairperson, Rajya Sabha, http://www.lawyerscollective.org/wp-content/uploads/2018/04/HC_orders_mothion.pdf.

44. The petition was ultimately withdrawn and no decision was handed down by the Court in this matter.

45. In Re: Matter of Great Public Importance Touching Upon the Independence of Judiciary, Suo Moto Writ Petition (Civil) No. 1/2019, decided on 20 April 2019. While Justice Gogoi sat on the bench and participated in the hearing, he did not sign the order.

46. See example, letter written by Senior Advocate Dushyant Dave to the judges of the Supreme Court alleging that even after Justice Gogoi assumed charge

as the Chief Justice of India, '[c]ases having far reaching consequences for the nation and the institution and cases involving political overtones, have been systematically assigned to benches "of preference" without any rational basis for such assignment'. Letter available at http://images.assettype.com/ barandbench/import/2019/08/Dushyant-Dave-letter.pdf. See also, Anup Surendranath, Aparna Chandra, & Suchindran Bhaskar Narayan, 'Justice Arun Mishra and the Supreme Court's Rule of Whim', Article 14, 5 September 2020, https://www.article-14.com/post/justice-arun-mishra-the-supreme-court-s-rule-of-whim.

47. See e.g., Lori Hausegger and Stacia Haynie, 'Judicial Decisionmaking and the Use of Panels in the Canadian Supreme Court and the South African Appellate Division', *Law and Society Review*, 37(3), pp. 635–658 (2003); Kaitlyn L. Sill and Stacia L. Haynie, 'Panel Assignment in Appellate Courts: Strategic Behaviour in the South African Supreme Court of Appeal', *Politikon*, 37:2–3, 269–285 (2010); Marin K. Levy and Adam S. Chilton, 'Challenging the Randomness of Panel Assignment in the Federal Courts of Appeals', 101 *Cornell Law Review* 1 (2015).

48. *Asok Pande v. Supreme Court of India*, (2018) 5 SCC 341.

49. *Shanti Bhushan v. Supreme Court of India*, (2018) 8 SCC 396.

50. See e.g., Manu Sebastian, 'Chief Justice of India Should Have No Power To Assign Cases To Benches, Allotment Must Be Automated: Dushyant Dave', LiveLaw, 11 August 2022, https://www.livelaw.in/top-stories/chief-justice-of-india-master-of-roster-power-to-assign-cases-to-bench-dushyant-dave-206289.

51. Balu Nair and Jai Brunner, 'Permanent Constitution Benches: Structural Reform of the Supreme Court', Supreme Court Observer, 4 October 2019, https://www.scobserver.in/journal/permanent-constitution-benches-structural-reform-of-the-supreme-court/.

52. On evading deciding cases, see Chapter 2.

53. On the challenges posed by automation in regulation of administrative decision-making, see 'Automated Decision Making and Administrative Law—A Nationwide Conversation on Law Reform', Australian Law Reform Commission, https://www.alrc.gov.au/news/automated-decision-making-and-administrative-law-a-nationwide-conversation-on-law-reform/; Frederik Zuiderveen Borgesius, 'Discrimination, Artificial Intelligence, and Algorithmic Decision-Making', Council of Europe, https://rm.coe.int/discrimination-artificial-intelligence-and-algorithmic-decision-making/1680925d73.

54. *Shanti Bhushan v. Supreme Court of India*, (2018) 8 SCC 396.
55. *Asok Pande v. Supreme Court of India*, (2018) 5 SCC 341.
56. Judges at the press conference seemed to suggest that there is an expectation within the Supreme Court that the most important matters will be heard by the senior-most judges. See also Abhinav Chandrachud, *Supreme Whispers: Conversations with Judges of the Supreme Court of India 1980-1989*, 20 (2018) (As Chief Justice of India, Justice Y. V. Chandrachud followed the seniority norm to avoid charges that he was 'stacking' cases for favourable outcomes). However, in *Asok Pande v. Supreme Court of India*, (2018) 5 SCC 341, the Supreme Court held that as co-equal judges on the bench, more 'senior' judges could not and should not be given such preference.

Chapter 5: People Like Us: Diversity (or Lack Thereof) in Judicial Appointments

1. The Constitution (Ninety-Ninth Amendment) Act, 2014, No. 49, Acts of Parliament, 1992 (India).
2. J. van Zyl Smit, 'The Appointment, Tenure and Remove of Judges Under Commonwealth Principles: A Compendium and Analysis of Best Practices', A Report of the Bingham Center for the Rule of Law, p. 30, Section 1.6 (2015).
3. The findings in this chapter are based on our own independent empirical analysis of relevant data. To understand our methodology and for more details on our findings, please see Aparna Chandra, William Hubbard and Sital Kalantry, 'From Executive Appointment to the Collegium System: The Impact on Diversity in the Indian Supreme Court', 51 *Verfassung und Recht in Übersee* 273 (2018).
4. Constitution of India, article 124.
5. Abhinav Chandrachud, *Supreme Whispers: Conversations with the Justices of the Supreme Court of India* (Gurgaon: PRHI, 2018).
6. M.P. Singh, 'Securing the Independence of the Judiciary—The Indian Experience', 10: 2 *The Indiana International & Comparative Law Review* 245, 265 (2000).
7. See *Kesavananda Bharati v. State of Kerala*, 4 SCC 225 (1973); *see also* Anil Divan, 'A Trojan Horse at the Judiciary's Door', *The Hindu*, 13 June 2016, https://www.thehindu.com/opinion/lead/a-trojan-horse-at-the-judiciarys-door/article4811353.ece.
8. *Additional District Magistrate, Jabalpur v. S.S. Shukla*, AIR 1976 SC 1207 (1976).

9. Maneesh Chhibber, 'In Remembering the Emergency, Don't Forget What Justice H.R. Khanna Wrote About Minorities', ThePrint, 2 July 2018, https://theprint.in/opinion/in-remembering-the-emergency-dont-forget-what-justice-h-r-khanna-wrote-about-minorities/77467/.

10. *S.P. Gupta v. President of India and Ors.*, AIR 1982 SC 149.

11. Ibid. at para. 29.

12. Ibid.

13. Constitution of India, article 217.

14. *S.P. Gupta v. President of India and Ors.*, AIR 1982 SC 149 (1982).

15. Abhinav Chandrachud, *Informal Constitution* (Oxford: Oxford University Press, 2014), pp. 112–115.

16. Ibid. at pp. 115–120.

17. *Supreme Court Advocates on Record Association v. Union of India*, (1993) 4 SCC 441.

18. *In re: Presidential Reference No. 1 of 1998*, 1998 7 SCC 739.

19. The Constitution (Ninety-Ninth Amendment) Act, 2014, No. 49, Acts of Parliament, 1992 (India).

20. The Constitution (Ninety-Ninth Amendment) Act, 2014, No. 49, Acts of Parliament, 1992 (India).

21. *Supreme Court Advocates on Record Association v. Union of India*, 2016 (5) SCC 1.

22. *Kesavananda Bharati v. State of Kerala*, 4 SCC 225 (1973), p. 316.

23. *Supreme Court Advocates on Record Association v. Union of India*, 2016 (5) SCC 1 at 325. But note there is some controversy among authors whether the majority of the judges clearly found that the basic structure of the Constitution required that judges must have the primary authority in appointment other judges. See e.g., Arghya Sengupta, 'A Legal Analysis of the NJAC Judgment: Judicial Primacy and the Basic Structure', 50:48 *Economic and Political Weekly* 27,27 (2015).

24. *Supreme Court Advocates on Record Association v. Union of India*, 2016 (5) SCC 1. At 314; *see also* Khagesh Guatam, 'Political Patronage and Judicial Appointments in India', 4 *Indonesian Journal of International & Comparative Law* 653 (2017), at 665.

25. *Supreme Court Advocates on Record Association v. Union of India*, 2016 (5) SCC 1 at 416.

26. Ibid. at 369.

27. Ibid. at 727–881.

28. See e.g., Rehan Abeyratne, 'Upholding Judicial Supremacy in India: The NJAC Judgment in Comparative Perspective', 49 *The George Washington International Law Review* 569, 576–579 (2016–2017).

29. Ibid. at 595–597

30. *Supreme Court Advocates on Record Association v. Union of India*, 2016 (5) SCC 1 at 791,792.

31. Ibid. at 508.

32. Ibid. at 1132.

33. Ibid.

34. Dhananjay Mahapatra, 'Collegium System: Don't Shoot the Messenger, It Will Hurt the Little Man's Faith in Judiciary', *Economic Times*, 12 September 2016, https://economictimes.indiatimes.com/news/politics-and-nation/collegium-system-dont-shoot-the-messenger-it-will-hurt-the-little-mans-faith-in-judiciary/articleshow/54288239.cms?from=mdr.

35. G.S. Vasu, 'Justice Chelameswar Skips SC Collegium Meet for Want of Transparency in Judges' Appointments', *New Indian Express*, 12 January 2018, http://www.newindianexpress.com/nation/2016/sep/02/tnie-exclusive-justice-chelameswar-skips-sc-collegium-meet-for-want-of-transparency-in-judges-appoin-1515267.html; Samanwaya Rautray, 'CJI Fails to Persuade Justice Chelameswar to Attend Collegium Meetings', *Economic Times*, 26 January 2017, https://economictimes.indiatimes.com/news/politics-and-nation/cji-fails-to-persuade-justice-chelameswar-to-attend-collegium-meetings/articleshow/56787406.cms?from=mdr.

36. Suhrith Parthasarathy, 'Collegium and Transparency', *The Hindu*, 1 November 2017, https://www.thehindu.com/opinion/lead/collegium-and-transparency/article19956961.ece.

37. See Supreme Court Resolutions, https://main.sci.gov.in/collegium-resolutions

38. See a recounting of these criticisms in the opinion of Justice Kurian (concurring) and Justice Chelameswar (dissenting) *in Supreme Court Advocates on Record Association v. Union of India*, 2016 (5) SCC 1.

39. Ibid.

40. Appu Suresh, 'Lost SC Berth for Opposing HC Judgeship for CJI Kabir's Sister: Guj CJ', *Indian Express*, 12 July 2013, https://indianexpress.com/article/news-archive/latest-news/lost-sc-berth-for-opposing-hc-judgeship-for-cji-kabirs-sister-guj-cj/.

41. SC Collegium gets woman member after over a decade, 5 April 2002, https://www.indiatoday.in/india/story/sc-collegium-gets-woman-member-after-over-decade-1619925-2019-11-18.

42. The Constitution (Ninety-Ninth Amendment) Act, 2014, No. 49, Acts of Parliament, 1992 (India).

43. Christina Boyd, Lee Epstein and Andrew Martin, 'On the Effective Communication of the Results of Empirical Studies, Part II', 60 *Vanderbilt Law Review* 801, 821 (2007).

44. 'OBCs Form 41 percent of Population: Survey', *Times of India*, 31 August 2007, https://timesofindia.indiatimes.com/india/OBCs-form-41-of-population-Survey/articleshow/2328117.cms.

45. The Constitution (One Hundred and Eighth Amendment) Bill, 2008 (India).

46. Although we collected data for all judges of the Supreme Court since its inception in 1950 when an executive-led system was in effect, our focus is on changes (if any) in the biographical characteristics of judges brought about by the change to the collegium system in 1993. For this reason, we focus only on the executive-led judges appointed since 1970—a time period that excludes judges who spent most of their careers in the colonial legal system as judges or lawyers (and who thus may systematically differ from judges appointed during the collegium system for reasons entirely unrelated to the collegium).

47. Religion Census 2011, http://www.census2011.co.in/religion.php.

48. Also, 15 per cent Indians are Muslim and the remaining people are Christian, Sikh, Buddhist and Jain. Ibid.

49. For example, of all the judges appointed under the executive-led system, 10 per cent were from the Allahabad High Court whereas, of all collegium-appointed judges, 5 per cent were from the Allahabad High Court. While it may appear that the executive is more likely to appoint judges from Allahabad High Court, there is no statistically significant difference between the appointments under the two systems. In making these calculations, we did not include the high courts from which no judges were appointed to the Supreme Court.

50. The fact that the people who were appointed by the executive and collegium are roughly proportional to the Indian religious and regional diversity, does not mean that at any one given time the Court was always representative of the Indian population. Our research describes only the overall distribution of judges who were appointed under both systems.

51. Scheduled Castes and Scheduled Tribes Population, http://censusindia.gov.in/Census_Data_2001/India_at_glance/scst.aspx.

52. Note we only include scheduled castes in our discussion rather than other backward classes.

53. Because our coding of high court data in the high court chief justices dataset was less consistent across coders than the coding of other variables in our data, we do not want to overemphasize this result, but we see this result as suggestive that, even among the most favoured group for appointment to the Court—high court Chief Justices—women appear to have a tougher path to the Supreme Court.

54. Pradeep Thakur, 'Approached Chief Justices of HCs for Appointments of More Dalit, Tribal Judges: Govt', *Times of India*, 15 March 2018, https://timesofindia.indiatimes.com/india/approached-chief-justices-of-hcs-for-appointments-of-more-dalit-tribal-judges-govt/articleshow/63322178.cms.

55. Alok Prasanna Kumar, 'Absence of Diversity in the Higher Judiciary', 51:8 *Economic and Political Weekly* (2016).

56. Rangin Pallav Tripathy, 'Fewer Indian Women in Higher Judiciary? Blame High Court Collegiums , Suggests Data', ThePrint, 22 July 2019, https://theprint.in/opinion/fewer-indian-women-in-higher-judiciary-blame-highcourt-collegiums-suggests-data/265747/.

57. Ibid.

58. Ibid.

59. Saurabh Kumar Mishra, 'Women in Indian Courts of Law: A Study of Women Legal Professionals in the District Court of Lucknow, Uttar Pradesh, India', available at https://journals.openedition.org/eces/1976, last accessed 30 October 2018.

60. Sheetal Sharma, 'Indian Women in the Legal Profession', Jawaharlal Nehru University (PhD Thesis) (2002), http://shodhganga.inflibnet.ac.in/bitstream/10603/29299/12/12_chapter per cent204.pdf, at 101.

61. 'Government releases data on number of women lawyers enrolled in country', Firstpost, 29 July 2022, https://www.firstpost.com/india/government-releases-data-on-number-of-women-lawyers-enrolled-in-country-10980711.html.

62. Alok Prasanna Kumar, *Absence of Diversity in the Higher Judiciary*, 51:8 *Economic and Political Weekly* (2016).

63. C. Raj Kumar, 'Future of Collegium System: Transforming Judicial Appointments for Transparency', 50:48 *Economic and Political Weekly*, November 2015.

64. For example, a 2010 study by Boyd, Epstein and Martin analysed 13 areas of decisions handed down by U.S. appellate courts, where judges hear and decide cases in panels of three. They found that in cases implying sex discrimination on the job, the probability of a judge deciding in favour of

the party alleging discrimination decreased by 10 percentage points when the judge was a male. Conversely, when a woman was on such a panel, the likelihood of a male judge ruling in favour of the plaintiff increased from 2 to 14 percent; Christina L. Boyd, Lee Epstein and Andrew D. Martin, 'Untangling the Causal Effects of Sex on Judging', *American Journal of Political Science* 54(2), 389-411(2010).

Chapter 6: Pandering to the Political Branches: Short Tenures and Early Retirements

1. See e.g., Arghya Sengupta, 'Former Chief Justice Gogoi's nomination to Rajya Sabha has cast doubt on the independence of India's judiciary', *Times of India*, last updated 20 March 2020, https://timesofindia.indiatimes.com/blogs/toi-edit-page/former-chief-justice-gogois-nomination-to-rajya-sabha-has-cast-doubt-on-the-independence-of-indias-judiciary/.

2. Pratap Bhanu Mehta, 'The Gogoi Betrayal: Judges Will Not Empower You, They Are Diminshed Men', *Indian Express*, last updated 20 March 2020, https://indianexpress.com/article/opinion/columns/ranjan-gogoi-supreme-court-rajya-sabha-6320869/?fbclid=IwAR0UF5EfbZ0bgdg79a4BZWxIBMCh62zj5Jgc14AVwiKhwYUW-i-WAjLMOfU.

3. Constitution of India, article 124, § 2 ('Every Judge of the Supreme Court shall be appointed by the President by warrant under his hand and seal after consultation with such of the Judges of the Supreme Court and of the High Courts in the States as the President may deem necessary for the purpose and shall hold office until he attains the age of sixty-five years[.]')

4. Madhav S. Aney, Shubhankar Dam and Giovanni Ko, 'Jobs for Justice(s): Corruption in the Supreme Court of India', 64 *Journal of Law and Economics* 479–511 (2021).

5. Ibid.

6. Constituent Assembly of India Debates (Proceedings), Volume VIII, 8.90.172–78, 24 May 1949, available at https://www.constitutionofindia.net/constitution_assembly_debates/volume/8/1949-05-24 [hereinafter 24 May 1949 Debate].

7. Constituent Assembly Debates, Constituent Assembly of India Debates (Proceedings), Volume X, 10.149.126, 12 October 1949, available at https://www.constitutionofindia.net/constitution_assembly_debates/volume/10/1949-10-12 [hereinafter October 12, 1949 Debate].

8. 24 May 1949 Debate, *supra* note 5, 8.90.24.

9. Memorandum representing the views of the federal court and of the Chief Justices representing all the provincial high courts of the Union of India, March 1948, in B. Shiva Rao, *The Framing of India's Constitution: Select Documents*, Vol IV 198–99 (1968).

10. 24 May 1949 Debate, *supra* note 5, 8.90.46.

11. Ibid., 8.90.47.

12. Ibid., 8.90.49.

13. See ibid., 8.100.50.

14. Ibid., 8.100.12.

15. Ibid., 8.90.50.

16. Ibid., 8.90.52.

17. Ibid., 8.90.141.

18. 24 May 1949 Debate, *supra* note 5, 8.90.39.

19. The Report of the Joint Committee on Indian Constitutional Reform (1934) proposed that the new Federal Court of India should have a retirement age of sixty-five. See Report of the Joint Committee on Indian Constitutional Reform, United Kingdom House of Commons, 323 (1 November 1934). Proposing a retirement age of sixty-five was a deliberate effort to have a higher retirement age for the Federal Court than for the Indian high courts (which had a retirement age of sixty) so as to incentivize high court judges to stay on as Federal Court judges: 'We have suggested that in the case of the Federal Court the age should be sixty-five, because it might otherwise be difficult to secure the services of High Court Judges who have shown themselves qualified for promotion to the Federal Court . . .' Ibid., 331.

20. Abhinav Chandrachud, 'The Need to Have a Uniform Retirement Age for Judges', 47 *Economic and Political Weekly* 24, 25–26 (2012). Chandrachud analyses the Joint Committee report to conclude that 'the five extra years of judicial service [between 60 and 65] were meant to serve as an incentive for retiring High Court judges to agree to serve on the Federal Court of India'. Ibid. at 25. He notes that '[t]he joint committee felt [. . .] a senior high court judge or a high court Chief Justice would be unwilling to give up his position of seniority and remaining years of service on an established court rather than take up a junior position on a new federal court with an uncertain future and tiny caseload'. Ibid.

21. Section 4 of the 1963 Constitution (Fifteen Amendment) Act amended Article 217 of the Constitution. *See* Constitution (Fifteenth Amendment) Act, 1963, Acts of Parliament 1963 (India), https://www.india.gov.in/my-

government/constitution-india/amendments/constitution-india-fifteenth-amendment-act-1963.

22. A Constitution Amendment Bill, brought by the previous UPA government, to increase the retirement age of high court judges to 65 to bring it at par with that of SC judges had lapsed with the dissolution of the 15th Lok Sabha in 2014, https://economictimes.indiatimes.com/news/politics-and-nation/government-not-to-fix-tenure-for-high-court-chief-justices/articleshow/51764246.cms.

23. World Bank, 'Life Expectancy at Birth, Total (Years)–India', last accessed 15 May 2020, https://data.worldbank.org/indicator/SP.DYN.LE00.IN?locations=IN.

24. Bagsmrita Bhagawati and Labananda Choudhury, 'Generation Life Table for India, 1901–1951', 12 *Middle East Journal of Age & Ageing* (2015).

25. Miqdad Asaria et al., 'Socioeconomic Inequality in Life Expectancy in India', *BMJ Global Health* (online) at 3, 5 (2019), https://gh.bmj.com/content/bmjgh/4/3/e001445.full.pdf.

26. Justices Kania, Hasan, Menon, Raj, Roy, Dwivedi, Mukerjee, Fasal Ali, Mukharji, Dayal, Patnaik and Srinivasan died in office before or during 2000.

27. Justice Shantanagoudar died in 2021.

28. Government of India Department of Justice, 'Revision of Salary and Pension of Judges, L-11017/1/2016-Jus.I, *Economic Times* Online, 30 January 2018; 'Supreme Court, High Court Judges Get Around 200 Per Cent Salary Hike', *Economic Times*, 30 January 2018, https://m.economictimes.com/news/politics-and-nation/supreme-court-24-high-court-judges-get-around-200-per-cent-salary-hike/articleshow/62712248.cms. For each completed year of service rendered as Chief Justice of a high court and as a judge, Supreme Court in addition to 3.1.1(i) above, taken together not exceeding Rs 15,00,000/- p.a. 3.1.2 Judges of the Supreme Court Rs 1,21,575/ House is quantified as 25 per cent of salary. 2.1.4.

29. Article 124 of the Constitution provides for the establishment and Constitution of the Supreme Court. Art. 124 § 7 provides: 'No person who has held office as a Judge of the Supreme Court shall plead or act in any court or before any authority within the territory of India'. See Constitution of India, *supra* note 3.

30. Abhinav Chandrachud, 'Time Has Come to Ask: Should Judges Stop Accepting Post-Retirement Jobs Offered By Govt', *Indian Express*, 18 March 2020, https://indianexpress.com/article/opinion/columns/former-

chief-justice-india-ranjan-gogoi-rajya-sabha-nomination-bjp-6319321/ [hereinafter *Post-Retirement Jobs*].

31. Ibid.; Abhinav Chandrachud, *The Informal Constitution* 70 (Oxford University Press, 2014).

32. 'The Government is the Biggest Litigant in the Country: SC Judge', *Indian Express*, 12 February 2015, https://indianexpress.com/article/india/india-others/government-is-the-biggest-litigant-in-the-country-sc-judge/.

33. Bingham Centre for the Rule of Law, 'The Appointment, Tenure and Removal of Judges Under Commonwealth Principles: A Compendium and Analysis of Best Practice', *British Institute of International and Comparative Law* 2.2.28 (2015) [hereinafter Bingham Centre Report].

34. Madhav S. Aney, Shubhankar Dam and Giovanni Ko, 'Jobs for Justice(s): Corruption in the Supreme Court of India', 64 *Journal of Law and Economics* 479–511 (2021).

35. Law Commission of India, *Fourteenth Report: Reform of Judicial Administration*, Volume 1, 39, 26 September 1958.

36. Ibid. at 39–40.

37. Law Commission of India, *Eightieth Report: The Method of Appointment of Judges*, 10 August 1979.

38. Burt Neuborne, 'The Supreme Court of India', 1 *International Journal of Constitutional Law* 476, 483 (2003).

39. Ibid.

40. George H. Gadbois Jr, 'Indian Supreme Court Judges: A Portrait', 3 *Law & Society Review* 317, 328 (1969).

41. The data for these calculations was found on https://main.sci.gov.in/chief-justice-judges.

42. Law Commission of India, *Fourteenth Report: Reform of Judicial Administration*, Volume 1, 37, 26 September 1958).

43. Christopher Sundby and Suzanna Sherry, 'Term Limits and Turmoil: Roe v. Wade's Whiplash', 98 *Texas Law Review* 121 (2019) (finding that if US Supreme Court judges had term limits, an important precedent on abortion, Roe v. Wade, would have changed over time).

44. Supreme Court Act, R.S.C. 1985, c. S-26, art 9(2) (Can.) https://laws-lois.justice.gc.ca/eng/acts/s-26/FullText.html.

45. Judicial Pensions and Retirement Act 1993, c. 26, § 4 (England and Wales), http://www.legislation.gov.uk/ukpga/1993/8/schedule/6/enacted?view=plain.

46. Bingham Centre Report, *supra* note 33, 2.2.14.

47. Ibid., 2.2.23.

48. The forty-three commonwealth countries include: Australia, the Bahamas, Bangladesh, Barbados, Belize, Botswana, Brunei, Cameroon, Canada, Cyprus, Fiji, Ghana, Guyana, India, Jamaica, Kenya, Lesotho, Malawi, Malaysia, Maldives, Malta, Mauritius, Mozambique, Namibia, Nauru, New Zealand, Nigeria, Organisation of Eastern Carribbean States (OECS), Pakistan, Papua New Guinea, Rwanda, Samoa, Seychelles, Sierra Leone, Singapore, Solomon Islands, South Africa, Sri Lanka, Swaziland, Tanzania, Trinidad and Tobago, Uganda, the United Kingdom, Vanuatu and Zambia.

49. The Indian Supreme Court shares the same retirement age with apex courts in Pakistan, Malawi, Malta, Sierra Leone, Trinidad and Tobago, Sri Lanka and Vanuatu.

50. See Bingham Centre Report, *supra* note 34, at 60.

51. Law Commission of India, *Report No. 230: Reforms in the Judiciary—Some Suggestions*, 11 (5 August 2009).

52. Law Commission of India, *Report No. 232: Retirement Age of Chairpersons and Members of Tribunals—Need For Uniformity*, 9 (August 2009).

53. Ibid.

54. Ibid., 2.2.29.

55. S. J. Sorabjee, 'Judges Should Not Be Given Post-Retirement Assignments', *Hindustan Times*, 7 February 1999. For other similar views see N. M. Ghatate, 'Ensuring Independence of Judges', 29 *Civil & Military Law Journal* 94, 96 (1993); Pratap Kumar Ghosh, *The Constitution of India: How it Has Been Framed* 240 (1966); Law Commission of India, *Fourteenth Report: Reform of Judicial Administration, supra* note 43, at 45.

56. 24 May 1949 Debate, *supra* note 6, 8.90.150.

57. *See* Chandrachud, *supra* note 31.

58. Arghya Sengupta and Ritwika Sharma, eds, *Appointment of Judges to the Supreme Court of India: Transparency, Accountability, and Independence* (Oxford University Press, 2018), 256.

59. Vinayak Madhubani, 'It will deprive the expectations of large number of aspirant lawyers who are very keen and ambitious for post of judgeship of High Court.', https://prsindia.org/files/bills_acts/bills_parliament/2010/SCR_Constitution_114th_Amendment_Bill,_2010.pdf.

Chapter 7: Conclusion: An Accountable Court

1. Upendra Baxi, 'Taking Suffering Seriously: Social Action Litigation in the Supreme Court of India' (1985) 4(1) *Third World Legal Studies* 107.

2. Ibid.

3. Nick Robinson, 'A Quantitative Analysis of the Indian Supreme Court's Workload', 10 *Journal of Empirical Legal Studies* 570, 574 (2013), p. 3.

4. See Chandra, Hubbard and Kalantry, 'The Supreme Court of India: An Empirical Overview of the Institution' *in A Qualified Hope: The Indian Supreme Court and Progressive Social Change,* ed. G. Rosenberg, S. Krishnaswamy and S. Bail, 43–76 (2019).

5. Madhav S. Aney, Shubhankar Dam and Giovanni Ko, *Jobs for Justice(s): Corruption in the Supreme Court of India*, 64 *Journal of Law and Economics,* 479–511 (2021).

Index